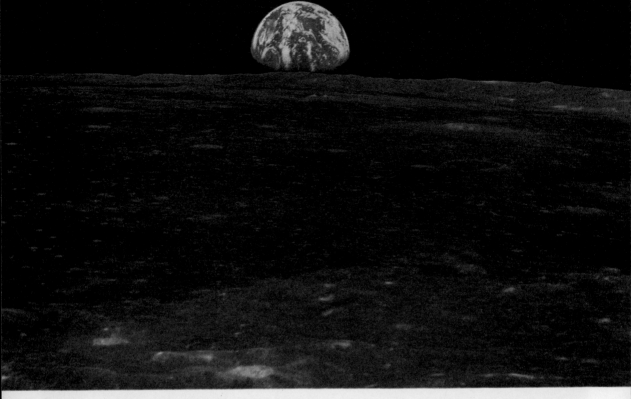

The earth, as seen from the moon 240,000 miles away, was photographed by the Apollo XI astronauts as their craft entered the lunar orbit prior to touchdown.
NASA

FRONT COVER: *Astronaut Edwin E. Aldrin, Jr. (top) stands beside the American flag that was planted on the moon on the first landing in 1969. The latest in down-to-earth air travel, the Boeing 747 (bottom left) can carry up to 362 passengers. President-elect Richard M. Nixon is briefed on national and international matters by President Lyndon B. Johnson (bottom right) before assuming office.*
NASA, PAN AMERICAN AIRLINES, UPI

FRONT ENDSHEET: *Probably the best known symbol of freedom in the entire world is the huge Statue of Liberty, which guards the entranceway to New York Harbor.*
PORT OF NEW YORK AUTHORITY

CONTENTS PAGE: *Earth Day, April 22, 1970, turned the nation's attention to a new issue —conservation. Here, demonstrators take over New York's Fifth Avenue.*
PHOTO TRENDS

BACK ENDSHEET: *The Capitol in Washington, D.C., is the national symbol of democracy. It is here that representatives of the 50 states meet to enact our laws.*
HERBERT LANKS, BLACK STAR

BACK COVER: *A helicopter brings in supplies (top) to an army outpost in Vietnam. Mounting war costs led to the first nationwide peace demonstrations (center right) in October, 1969. Martin Luther King reaches the Alabama State Capitol (center left) after his historic civil-rights march in 1965. Shown together at Speaker Sam Rayburn's funeral in 1961 are (bottom) former Presidents Harry S. Truman and Dwight D. Eisenhower with President John F. Kennedy.*
UPI, UPI, PHOTO TRENDS, UPI

AMERICAN HERITAGE
NEW ILLUSTRATED HISTORY
OF THE UNITED STATES

VOLUME 16

AMERICA TODAY

CREATED AND DESIGNED BY THE EDITORS OF
AMERICAN HERITAGE
The Magazine of History

PUBLISHED BY FAWCETT PUBLICATIONS, INC.
ONE ASTOR PLAZA, NEW YORK, N.Y. 10036

CONTENTS OF THE COMPLETE SERIES

Foreword by JOHN F. KENNEDY
Introduction by ALLAN NEVINS
Main text by ROBERT G. ATHEARN

EACH VOLUME CONTAINS AN ENCYCLOPEDIC SECTION; MASTER INDEX IN THIS VOLUME

CONTENTS OF VOLUME 16

1354

CHAPTER 46

THE COLD WAR

The war was over. Armed forces that had at their peak numbered more than 12,300,000 were coming home—first in a trickle, then in a flood. The strongest, best-equipped fighting force in the history of the nation shrank to a military establishment of about 1,500,000 by 1947. The industrial might of the country spun on its axis to meet the pent-up domestic needs of a population that had lived for four long years with shortages and rationing. There were cars and trucks to be built and bought, highways and bridges and tunnels to be constructed. There was housing to be erected, appliances and consumer goods to be manufactured and marketed. There were factories to be refurbished, priorities to be overhauled.

The nation faced the enormous task of converting from a wartime to a peacetime economy. Price and wage controls had to be lifted, but without touching off an inflationary spiral. Military advances in technology had to be diverted to domestic uses. American industry looked covetously to the enormous new pool of manpower that would quickly be at its disposal. Congress looked, too, and Congress worried, recalling the labor glut that had sent veterans of World War I into the streets selling apples in the 1920s. Nevertheless, there was a spirit of optimism abroad in the country. Resources in the United States were unparalleled. Personal and corporate savings were at an all-time high. They represented a pool of capital easily tapped to finance the conversion. Demand for goods and services was increasing, not only in America, where there was money to satisfy demand, but in war-torn Europe and Asia, where there was not. International credits needed to be established. Economies abroad would have to be rebuilt. Demand was an asset to the nation that could meet it, and America was not only the

The Wall—grim symbol of the cold war —was built in 1961 to prevent East Germans from escaping to freedom in West Berlin. It is 29 miles long and 8 to 12 feet high. Here it seals off the Brandenburg Gate from the British sector. The barbed wire is to keep West Berliners out of a no man's land.

sole major industrial power fully intact at the close of the war, but also had made vast productive strides during it.

Conversely, unsatisfied demand was also a serious threat to the peace and security of the world. From this simple economic proposition emerged two basic goals that shaped and guided the foreign and domestic policies of the United States for the first 15 postwar years: (1) the need to prevent another worldwide conflagration and (2) the need to prevent an economic collapse. They were the goals of a mature and responsible world power, confident of its political and economic ability to satisfy the expectations of its own people. Indeed, these twin goals still inform much of the nation's policy. After World War II, the nation that had sought in 1920 to "return to normalcy" and a kind of economic status quo now endorsed the concept of a broadening middle class and a wider sharing of national wealth. The nation that had rejected the League of Nations in 1919 now embraced the need of a worldwide peace-keeping organization of all nations.

The nation's confidence was high. America had the resources, the technology, and the manpower. It had the means and the will to build and maintain a prosperous peace. Moreover, it had the most terrifying weapon in the world to enforce peace, the atomic bomb. Who would dare to threaten war? The United States and her Western allies soon got a startling answer.

Struggle in Europe

Joseph Stalin, dictator of the Soviet Union, saw the postwar scene in a different light. His nation was in partial ruin, yet stronger than it had ever been as the result of new defense plants erected during the conflict. The United States, driven by the need of an ally to engage Hitler's war machine from the east, had helped to "seed" Russia with the capital and tools to build a modern war potential of her own. In making the transition from war production to peacetime industrialization, Russia could not expect to compete in the international markets with the Americans, but she could isolate from the West a number of those markets in Europe and Asia. The Soviet Union set out to do so.

Eastern Europe was the first target of opportunity. It offered both markets and a manufacturing tradition—particularly East Germany, Czechoslovakia, Poland, and Hungary. As a result of wartime agreements with the Allies, Russia already occupied all of Eastern Europe. Maintaining their occupying armies there, the Russians proceeded by a combination of military presence and internal political penetration to establish Communist regimes, with close ties to Soviet economic and military policy. The gateways of trade be-

Among the Communist leaders attending the celebration of Joseph Stalin's 70th birthday in Moscow in 1950 were Mao Tse-tung, Nikita Khrushchev, and Vyacheslav Molotov.

tween Eastern and Western Europe slammed shut, prompting Winston Churchill, Britain's wartime Prime Minister, to comment in 1946: "An iron curtain has descended across the Continent." By 1948, the Communists had seized power in Albania, Bulgaria, Czechoslovakia, East Germany, Hungary, Poland, Rumania, and Yugoslavia. Powerful Communist parties, built around the nuclei of partisan underground fighters, were gaining influence in France and in Italy; and Russia was gazing rapaciously toward Greece and strategic Turkey, the key to control of the eastern Mediterranean. Thus, the stage was set for a worldwide confrontation of capitalist and communist systems.

The industrial powers of Europe, including Britain, were exhausted by the war. If Stalin's territorial aims for communism were to be contained, the United States would have to act. But America, once in such a hurry to win the war, was now preoccupied with domestic problems. Demobilization became the first concern of the country. An elaborate "point system," which took into account length of service, length of time in a combat theater, military awards, and service-connected disabilities, ruled the mustering-out process. It was designed to avert the abrupt weakening of the armed forces, as well as to prevent returning servicemen from overpowering industry with job demands. The system was equitable; however, many believed it to be much too slow. At the urging of President Harry S. Truman, Congress enacted other measures to ease the demobilization. There was a one-year unemployment bonus of $20 per week available for each qualified ex-serviceman unable to find work. Hundreds of thousands took advantage of this bonus, partly as a respite from the activities of war, largely as a necessary compensation until they could find suitable jobs. Perhaps the most enlightened measure was the offer of free tuition and maintenance for returning servicemen who wanted to continue their education. Veterans by the millions returned to school. Intended primarily to blunt the effect of demobilization, this single government program became the root of vast sociological change and great economic advances. In the decade between 1940 and 1950, before the impact of postwar population growth was felt in the classroom, school enrollment rose by more than 1,500,000. It had risen by less than 100,000 in the preceding decade. The example of mature young men delaying the beginning of their work careers and struggling, often with young families, to better themselves touched off an education boom. This, in turn, was to provide the industrial, commercial, and professional sectors of the nation with a higher degree of literacy and competence than ever before. As a result, 20 years after the war the educational level of the average American had risen a full three years. The average American adult in 1945 had a grade-school education with one year of high school. By 1965, the typical American was a high school graduate, and the illiteracy rate was down to 2.4% of the adult population.

The price of peace

In the immediate postwar years, however, gaps in educational and economic opportunities available to Americans became visible. President Truman sought to press civil-rights legislation; however, together with attempts to deal with many of the other dislocations of the conversion from war to peace, the effort was to carry a high political price. Shortages among various goods and commodities continued through 1946. Truman fought for continuing price controls in certain important areas of the economy. However, the mood of the country argued against him. America had had enough of regulation, and as price controls vanished, consumer prices began to rise. Organized labor reacted with demands for higher wages, and the result was a series of crippling strikes beginning in late 1945 that one time or another over the next two years closed down much or all of the nation's automobile, coal, railroad, airline, steel, shipping, and meatpacking industries.

The public wrath was directed at Truman. He was blamed for the grinding pace of demobilization, for the shortages in consumer goods, for the various dislocations that inevitably occur when a nation leaves the warpath and turns to peace. To the Democratic Party went the blame for the seemingly unlimited power of labor to strike crippling blows at the important areas of the nation's economy. Many felt that the culprit legislation was the 1935 National Labor Relations Act (Wagner Act), which strongly backed the right of labor to organize and bargain collectively. The Republicans skillfully exploited the argument that this law gave labor too much power. "Had enough?" demanded the G.O.P. publicists. The pendulum of American political opinion appeared to be swinging back to the right, after 14 years of social reform.

The Congressional elections of 1946 tended to confirm this. They were a Democratic disaster. After enjoying comfortable majorities in both houses of the 79th Congress, the Democrats tumbled ingloriously to minority roles in each. They lost nine seats in the Senate, giving the Republicans a 51-to-45 majority; and they lost an unprecedented 54 seats in the House, providing a 245-to-189 Republican majority there.

Publicly undismayed, Truman continued to press for modest civil-rights legislation, and he took up the fight against what many labor leaders felt to be retaliatory labor legislation.

French farmers learn to use up-to-date American-built tractors sent as part of the 1947 Marshall Plan to help revitalize the economy of Europe.

Children stand on what remains of a bombed building in Berlin in 1948 to watch an American plane delivering its cargo of coal in the Berlin airlift.

He lost on both issues. Few new social-reform measures were enacted, and a new labor law—the Taft-Hartley Act of 1947—was passed over Truman's veto. This measure outlawed the "closed shop" that had prevented a union plant from hiring nonunion personnel. It restricted the union shop, which had obligated workers to join the resident union within a set period of time. The new law also enabled the government to delay a strike for an 80-day "cooling off" period if the national interest was threatened.

Balked in his domestic program by a strong conservative coalition in Congress, Truman still managed to carry on a vigorous and far-sighted foreign policy. Alert now to the dangers of a power vacuum in Europe, the United States proclaimed in March, 1947, a policy of military and economic aid to nations threatened by Soviet ambitions. Later called the Truman Doctrine, this policy was basically designed to contain communism. As a start, $400,000,000 in aid was allocated to Greece and Turkey. Three months later, in June at Harvard University, Secretary of State George C. Marshall proposed a vast program of aid for the free nations of Europe (the European Recovery Program) to help rebuild their shattered economies. The Marshall Plan, the first in the history of the world to offer economic assistance to friends and former foes alike, was to become the first and the most successful of American foreign-aid programs. Funded by more than $12,000,000,-000 in American economic aid, industry, agriculture, and mineral production in Western Europe revived, and the free nations began to draw new breath of their own.

Russia's reaction to these initiatives was to abrogate the four-power agreement of free access to Berlin. In June, 1948, the Soviets blockaded the land and water routes into Germany's old capital city, 110 miles inside the Russian zone. No amount of diplomatic persuasion nor world opinion could remove the roadblocks. The aim was to force the Western powers to give up their occupation zones in Berlin. The West responded with one of the strangest supply operations in history. Throwing together a collection of C-47 and C-54 cargo planes, the United States airlifted potatoes, coal, meat, vegetables, and all of the other staples of a modern city into Berlin's Tempelhof Airport. For 24 hours a day seven days a week for more than ten months, the supplies poured into the blockaded city. The Russians, beaten at their gambit, finally re- moved the roadblocks in May, 1949. But by that time, the nations on both sides of the North Atlantic rim had pooled their armed forces in a joint command under the new North Atlantic Treaty Organization (NATO) to provide a military presence to counter the Russian divisions in Eastern Europe. As the stalemate deepened abroad, American attention was diverted again to domestic issues.

An upset victory

Meanwhile, the 1948 Presidential elections had taken place. The effect of Truman's remarkable performance in Europe was not yet manifest to the electorate at home by the time of the voting, and NATO had not yet been officially established. Moreover, many of the President's domestic programs had failed to get through Congress. A Republican victory seemed to be in the air. Truman's espousal of civil rights and his fight against the Taft-Hartley Act had lost him the support of the conservative Southern leadership. On the other hand, his failure to move Congress with a middle-of-the-road approach cost him the support of the progressive wing of his party. As November approached, the Southerners formed a states' rights (or "Dixiecrat") faction and bolted the Democratic Convention to nominate Strom Thurmond, governor of South Carolina, for President. The liberal wing formed the Progressive

It was Truman's hard campaigning, much of it at whistle stops like this one in Idaho (above), that gave him his victory in 1948. The day after election, he gleefully displayed the Chicago Tribune's *premature headline (below).*

Party and nominated former Vice-President Henry A. Wallace.

The Republicans confidently selected New York Governor Thomas E. Dewey, and the party and its candidate settled back to await the inevitable victory. As the campaign began, Dewey avoided specific expressions on issues and ran as a statesman. In the opinion of the pundits, he was a certain winner. Cast in the role of the underdog, Harry Truman soon became the hardest-fighting underdog to stride across the Presidential campaign scene in modern times. Denied for the most part the editorial support of the nation's press, he took his campaign to the grass roots and, crisscrossing the country, the President denounced the Republican 80th Congress as a "do-nothing Congress." He elaborated with specifics, charging the Republicans with the responsibility for everything that was wrong with life in these United States. "Give 'em hell, Harry!" was a frequent response from the large crowds drawn to his spirited campaign. Labor rallied to him, and he raced back and forth across the Midwestern wheat and corn belts in a special train, hardly missing a whistle-stop in a determined bid to unify the farm vote. In one of the most stunning upsets of American political history, Truman carried 28 states with 303 electoral votes, Dewey carried 16 states with 189, and the states' rights Dixie-crats, four Southern states with 39.

Now elected President in his own right, Truman sought to press his Fair Deal program of social-reform measures, but the Democratic 81st Congress, while it did seek to modify some of the more stringent passages of the new Taft-Hartley Act, was little more responsive to the President's wishes than the Republican 80th. The man from Missouri who entered the Presidency with few pretensions of greatness was again to find his role cast on a global scale.

Global competition

Although Communist expansion in Europe had apparently reached its highwater mark with the Berlin blockade, Communist power and prestige were by no means waning. The West was to receive three damaging blows in three years, each more shaking than its predecessor. In 1949, Russia exploded an atomic bomb. Up until this moment, Stalin's ambitions had always been tempered by his knowledge that he risked a shooting war in Europe at great peril to Russia. But with atomic arms in Soviet hands, America's monopoly of the "ultimate weapon" was effectively checked, and the tentative peace of Europe could be threatened once again by the superior numbers under arms behind the Iron Curtain. It was a rude awakening for Americans accustomed to believing that Russia, while strong, was no technological match for the United

Chinese workers march in the National Day Parade, October 1, 1950, commemorating the first anniversary of Mao Tse-tung's Communist regime.

States. It had become fashionable to believe that the Soviets, in one popular phrase, "could not produce a decent flush toilet." The Soviets had in little more than four years duplicated the world's highest technological achievement, the release of atomic energy. Of course, the U.S.S.R. had had the services of captured German scientists as well as the aid of skilled and highly organized espionage agents who had penetrated the atomic arsenal of the West. Public opinion might console itself with that inside the United States. To the rest of the world, however, a new superpower had arrived. To cope with the new threat, NATO was strengthened. Eventually it would grow to 51 divisions, backed up with American-equipped air support and the U.S. Sixth Fleet prowling the Mediterranean.

The next blow fell in Asia. Communist revolutionaries had been fighting for control of China since long before World War II. With the emergence of Chiang Kai-shek's

Nationalists from the ruins of Sun Yat-sen's Republic, the Communists under Mao Tse-tung retreated more than 1,000 miles into the remote interior, there to await their time. It came at the close of World War II. With Japan defeated and withdrawn from the Asian mainland, Mao struck. In four years, he brought Chiang's Nationalists to decisive battle and drove them out of China, across the Formosan Strait to the island of Formosa, which they renamed Taiwan. With American aid, Chiang turned Taiwan into a military and industrial stronghold. Free China's presence was further maintained at the United Nations, where Chiang's government held the fifth seat on the U.N. Security Council. But Communists controlled a more tangible Asian reality—one sixth of the world's surface, one fourth of the world's population. To the uncommitted nations the nuclear feat and the territorial accomplishment were impressive performances. The last of the three blows was struck in Asia also.

War in Korea

On June 25, 1950, North Korean troops stormed across the 38th parallel that divided Communist north from non-Communist south on this formerly Japanese-controlled peninsula. They quickly drove through the thinly deployed South Korean troops and pushed them and their American advisors into a shallow perimeter around the southern port city of Pusan. The American response was immediate. U.S. troops in Japan and the Philippines were rushed to the embattled perimeter. The United States sought and got—because the Russians were engaging in one of their periodic boycotts of the Security Council—United Nations support of the military response. General of the Army Douglas MacArthur was placed in command of U.N. forces. Contingents from other nations were mobilized. MacArthur mounted a brilliant amphibious attack on Inchon, more than halfway up the South Korean coast. The offensive cut the communications of the North Koreans and drove them north in disarray, almost to the Yalu River, which separates North Korea from Mainland China. The U.N. Command spoke of having the troops home by Christmas, but the Communists were not done yet. Thirty-three divisions of Chinese regulars, masquerading as "volunteers," poured across the Yalu. In a series of massive infantry assaults, the Chinese pushed the U.N. forces halfway down the Korean peninsula again and crossed the 38th parallel before MacArthur's troops were able to check their advance. The war settled into a bloody stalemate. Then, Truman dramatically relieved MacArthur in the spring of 1951. America's most popular warrior and the President had been clashing on the overall conduct of the war for months. MacArthur wanted to use all possible means to win it.

Documents in the dispute are still classified. MacArthur, however, is known to have advocated attacking Chinese territory, and it has been suggested that he wanted to use nuclear weapons. Truman wanted to avoid at all costs an open war with China, which would have involved committing American forces to the vast Asian mainland as a first step and would, as a second, have provoked, perhaps beyond settlement, a nuclear confrontation with Russia herself. MacArthur submitted quietly to recall, allowing his many admirers in Congress and in the press to do his speaking for him. In an address to a joint session of Congress, he skirted the specifics of the dispute and in a moving peroration foretold his eclipse: "Old soldiers," he concluded in his husky baritone, "never die, they just fade away."

The old soldier carried the emotional day. However, the President had reinforced the principle of civilian authority over the military. The war dragged on, domestic problems multiplied, high-level scandals of influence peddling rocked the Truman administration, and grave doubts arose concerning the internal se-

In snow and freezing weather, a machine gun—set into a Korean hill facing the Communist forces—is about to be fired by American soldiers.

curity of the United States. Truman announced early in 1952 that he would not be a candidate for re-election, and the Democrats chose the liberal and highly accomplished governor of Illinois, Adlai E. Stevenson, as their candidate. However, it was clearly "time for a change." Truman's election of 1948 was judged as more of a performance of political virtuosity than an expression of the mood of the country, which was still looking for a respite from conflict, both foreign and domestic. The Republicans were taking no chances. They nominated the immensely popular Dwight D. Eisenhower, World War II Supreme Commander of Allied forces in Europe, the postwar president of Columbia University, and, after December, 1950, commander of the Supreme Headquarters of Allied Powers in Europe (SHAPE), NATO's armed forces. The Korean War and the global Communist threat occupied stage center of the 1952 Presidential campaign. Eisenhower trod gingerly around the thorny problem of conducting limited warfare in a nuclear age. He suggested that he would bring the conflict in Korea to an end after making on-the-site evaluations. "IKE WILL GO TO KOREA" said the headlines, and Americans, in their frustration with the war, were comforted by the thought of this sincere man applying his knowledge and experience as Commander-in-Chief.

While fulfilling a campaign promise to make an inspection tour of Korea, Eisenhower eats with men from the front.

He won 442 electoral votes to the hapless Stevenson's 89. A Republican Congress accompanied him to power.

Eisenhower began his administration with high energy, convinced that he could bring order and responsiveness to the vast confusion of interests that had increased with the growth of the federal establishment over 20 years of Democratic administration. "Poor Ike," commented Harry Truman. "He'll say, 'Do this' and 'Do that' and nothing will happen." Truman was to prove largely correct. The collision of the high-powered army general and inertia-bound bureaucracy shot off an occasional spark, but it hardly altered the working pace or the size of big government. Too many interests contended for attention in the formulation and execution of federal policy.

Peace is achieved

Foremost of Eisenhower's problems was the Korean War. Armistice talks had actually begun in July, 1951, at Kaesong and had been moved that October to the small border village of Panmunjom. They dragged on with interruptions for two years. Eisenhower made his inspection tour of Korea with little effect other than a marked rise in morale. But finally, on July 26, 1953, armistice terms were agreed to, and the shooting ended 12 hours later. The Asian Communists were not to follow the Korean example of conventional battleline warfare again. Two thousand miles south of Korea, the French, trying to hold on to their old colonial possessions in Indochina, were threatened by Ho Chi Minh. In the spring of 1954, Ho's forces drew the French into the valley stronghold of Dien Bien Phu in North Vietnam and on May 8 defeated them decisively. Vietnam was partitioned along the 17th parallel, and thereafter the defense of the South and its government was to become increasingly an American responsibility. After Dien Bien Phu, the United States established with seven other nations the South East Asia Treaty Organization (SEATO). It was never to gain the strength of its Atlantic counterpart, NATO, and the multinational commitments to SEATO—aside from continuing American presence in Far Eastern military bases resulting from the 1948 Treaty of San Francisco with Japan—were no match to NATO.

The American public, after the close of the Korean War, paid little attention to these moves. They were more concerned with the growing controversy over internal security and civil liberties. Beginning in 1948, the United States was to pass through nearly seven years of domestic uproar over the amount of influence exercised by Communists or fellow travelers on U.S. policy. The denunciation of Alger Hiss, once a trusted advisor in the State Department, as an agent for Russia touched off the issue. Hiss denied specific charges leveled at him by former Communist Whittaker Chambers but was convicted two years later of perjury. The issue, originally raised in the House Un-American Activities Committee, was fanned to white heat in 1950 with the emergence of an obscure Midwestern Senator, Joseph R. McCarthy (Republican, Wisconsin) who claimed but never proved that he had a list of 205 Communists in the Department of State. Having gained prominence with his charge, McCarthy next gained power to exploit it when the Republican 83rd Congress took office in 1953.

The end of the investigations by Joseph McCarthy (left) came in 1954 when many Senators, like Ralph Flanders (right), began to criticize his methods.

As the ranking Republican on the Senate Committee on Government Operations, he became its chairman. He also took over the chairmanship of its subcommittee on investigations, and from this position he launched a series of hearings and investigations that had the effect of suggesting that the government was riddled from top to bottom with Communists and their sympathizers. To mounting demands that he be required to prove, not merely state his charges, the country split into pro-McCarthy and anti-McCarthy camps. The issue grew venomous when McCarthy's camp began equating anti-McCarthyism with pro-Communism. McCarthy himself burst this overinflated bubble. In 1953, he attacked General George C. Marshall, former Secretary of State, as a Communist agent. Eisenhower, aloof but concerned as the controversy grew less reasonable, defended his former chief. McCarthy's reaction—incredible as it might seem—was to suggest that Eisenhower himself was somehow in league with the Communists. As the

1369

This giant statue of Joseph Stalin was toppled by students and workers in Budapest on October 23, 1956, the day that the Hungarian revolt began.

Wisconsin Senator's credibility waned, the Senate convened a special committee to investigate charges brought by the army as the result of the Senator's inquiry into subversive activities. Following the so-called Army-McCarthy hearings, which were televised nationally, the Senate, on December 2, 1954, voted 67 to 22 to condemn him for abuse of the Senate and insults to its members. McCarthy's power and the fear his methods had stitched into the politics of the early 1950s were over.

Meanwhile, the uneasy peace of Europe survived a series of crises. The sinister hegemony of Joseph Stalin over the Communist world had ended with his death in March, 1953. New initiatives were taken between East and West. In February, 1956, Stalin's ultimate successor, Nikita S. Khrushchev, in a three-hour speech to the 20th Congress of the Communist Party, denounced Stalin as a tyrant, repudiated the Stalinist purges of the 1930s, and proclaimed a policy of peaceful—but competitive—coexistence with the West. The old Stalinists, notably Lavrenti P. Beria, head of the secret police, had already been purged from the government. Beria himself was executed in 1953 after an unsuccessful grab for power. Hardly had the world's spirits begun to lift, however, when a new series of crises gripped Europe and the Middle East. In October, 1956, Hungarian students and workers revolted against the Communist regime. Russian garrison troops, at least partly in sympathy with the Hungarian masses, withdrew from the Hungarian capital of Budapest, but seven days later, fresh Soviet occupying forces, drawn largely from behind the Urals, brutally crushed the revolt. The United States could not intervene. The Truman Doctrine did not extend behind the Iron Curtain. But beyond the question of policy lay the terrifying prospect of thermonuclear war. In 1952, the United States had successfully tested the hydrogen bomb and begun to build up her arsenal of these awesome weapons.

The Russians were less than a year behind with their H-bomb, and intercontinental-ballistic delivery systems were on the horizon.

The Hungarian revolt was still in progress when flames erupted in the Middle East. The new state of Israel, smarting over growing Arab hostility and Egypt's seizure from the British of the vital Suez Canal on July 26, 1956, launched an attack on Egypt's Sinai Peninsula through the Gaza Strip. Britain and France intervened on Israel's side, and the U.N. demanded a cease-fire. The United States supported the U.N. demand and condemned the attack, a surprising move on the surface. But the action was an expression of increasing concern by Eisenhower and Secretary of State John Foster

The year after their first political contest Adlai E. Stevenson was the guest of honor at this White House luncheon hosted by President Eisenhower.

UNITED PRESS INTERNATIONAL

Dulles for stability in this strategic and oil-rich region. The Arab world was being actively wooed by the Soviets. If Russia could establish Communist domination here, she would control one sixth of the world's oil resources and stand athwart the gateway between Europe and the Far East. In January, 1957, President Eisenhower took steps to protect what he considered America's vital interests in the Middle East. He issued the Eisenhower Doctrine, a new policy declaring that the United States would give economic aid and would use "armed force" to protect any country in the area from Communist aggression. In May, 1958, that policy was tested when pro-Egyptian forces, backed by the Soviet Union, threatened the Lebanese government. Eisenhower ordered marines into Lebanon and kept them there at the request of the government for a full month until internal stability was restored.

Balance of terror

By this time, international peace had poised delicately for nearly a decade upon a wave of continuing crisis, and the old European imperative for peace—a balance of power —began to give way to a new concept: World peace was not only *threatened* but also *protected* by the terror of nuclear warfare. Equilibrium was being maintained, despite crises, by the unwillingness of either superpower to risk a nuclear strike, because it feared a counterstrike. In short, there existed a balance of terror.

Beneath this fearsome umbrella the principal underlying goal of the United States, the prevention of another major war, was being achieved. The major domestic goal, prevention of another economic depression, was also weathering well. During the decade of the 1950s, the nation sustained an average economic growth rate of approximately 3.2% annually. A recession occurred in 1956–57, but pump priming by the Eisenhower administration— largely in the form of a massive federally supported highway building program—quickly restored the upward movement of the economy.

Eisenhower had handily won re-election in 1956, beating Adlai Stevenson again, this time by an electoral margin of 457 to 73. But for the first time in 108 years, an American President would not carry into office with him a majority in either of the two houses of Congress. The election was a tribute to the great popularity of Eisenhower the man. But new forces were stirring in the land. A new generation of leaders, "born in this century," was rising, and new national goals, concerned as much with quality as with quantity, were beginning to take form. They would give rise in time to two internal revolutions, one social, the other technological. Both of them would lead to profound changes in the America of the next decade.

NATIONAL AERONAUTICS AND SPACE ADMINISTRATION

THE WORLD
OF OUTER SPACE

Just as man was once impelled to explore the seas and search for lands, so he has reached out into the world beyond his own planet. From the early days of unmanned space probes in the late 1950s (when rockets such as the Juno II, above, were launched) until July 20, 1969, when man first stepped on the moon's surface, thousands of technicians around the globe have contributed to the conquest of the "unknown." Although the program to put man in space and on the moon has received the most attention, many other achievements have occurred that seemed impossible when the National Aeronautics and Space Administration was created in 1958—weather observations and intercontinental communications for orbiting satellites, to mention but a few. Still, man is not content: Research continues, and one day he will explore new worlds that today seem well beyond his reach.

THE RUSSIANS ACHIEVED
MANY SPACE "FIRSTS"

Most of the initial successes in space exploration belonged to the Russians, who rightfully took great pride in their accomplishments. Above the Soviet magazine *Krokodil* salutes the world's first space hero, Yuri Gagarin, for his pioneering orbit of the earth on April 12, 1961. In August of that same year Gherman S. Titov made 16 orbits; in 1962, two other Russians made 45 and 60 orbits in a double flight. The cosmonauts were given highest honors and sent on tours of both the Soviet Union and foreign countries to call attention to Russia's achievements and lead in the early days of the space age.

The Russians inaugurated the space age when Sputnik I was launched on October 4, 1957. The first man-made object to be put into orbit, it circled the earth at distances up to 560 miles for three months. In the picture above, taken in East Germany a model of it is on the left; at right is the much more elaborate Sputnik III, which was launched in 1958.

Cosmonaut Gagarin is shown just before take-off. His flight took him in an orbit 108 to 187 miles out, and he reached a top speed of some 17,000 miles an hour—the fastest man had traveled up to that time.

Valentina V. Tereshkova, 26—a former textile worker whose parachuting hobby led her into the Russian space program— was the first woman to orbit the earth, 48 times in just 70 hours and 50 minutes.

MIGHTIEST BOOSTER

Almost from the start of the space race with Russia, the United States set its sights on landing men on the moon. To do so required the development of a rocket capable of carrying a manned craft across 240,000 miles of space and back again. After nearly a decade of work, the three-stage, multiengine Saturn V (being test-fired at right) was perfected. Although the Titan II (seen at left launching Gemini X into earth orbit in 1966) can generate 430,000 pounds of thrust to lift 8,000 pounds into earth orbit, the first stage of the Saturn (below) produces 7,500,000 pounds of thrust.

AMERICA SENDS ITS ASTRONAUTS ALOFT

ALL: NASA

Months of training and testing preceded the first phase of America's manned space program—Project Mercury. Ground simulators, such as the one at left, prepared astronauts for manually controlling their spacecrafts. Pictured here are three U.S. space pioneers: above, Colonel John H. Glenn, Jr., the first American to orbit the earth; below left, Commander Walter M. Schirra, Jr.; below right, Major L. Gordon Cooper, Jr.

PREPARING FOR THE MOON

If man was to be able to work in space, and not merely revolve in it—a prerequisite for a lunar landing—he had to prove that he could maneuver both himself and his craft while aloft. These were among the objectives of Project Gemini, the second step in America's moon program. From March 23, 1965, until November 11, 1966, ten Gemini flights, each with two astronauts aboard, were launched from the NASA "spaceport" at Cape Kennedy, Florida. Many new records were set: the first manned orbital maneuvers, by Virgil I. Grissom and John W. Young in Gemini III; the first extended manned flight (120 revolutions in eight days), by the Gemini V crew; and the docking of a spacecraft with an orbiting target, by Neil A. Armstrong and David R. Scott aboard Gemini VIII.

ALL: NASA

Thousands of scientists, engineers, and technicians make up the American space team that guides manned flights from 15 NASA installations. Above is a firing room in the Launch Control Center at Cape Kennedy during a before-flight test for Apollo IX.

From 160 miles above the earth Gemini VII (left) is seen through the hatch window of Gemini VI as they rendezvous in December, 1965. Below, Edward H. White II has his picture taken by Gemini IV command pilot James A. McDivitt during his spectacular 21-minute "walk in space" on June 3, 1956. White, though, was not the first man ever to move about in space from an orbiting craft; Russian cosmonaut Aleksei A. Leonov had performed the same feat only three months earlier.

PROJECT APOLLO

In May, 1961, President John F. Kennedy officially committed America to landing a man on the moon and returning him safely to earth "before this decade is out." After a score of successful manned missions, Project Apollo—the final phase of the lunar program—achieved fulfillment. On July 16, 1969, the crew of Apollo XI began their epic-making journey, a trip soon to become common-place. Aboard were (below, left to right) Neil A. Armstrong, commander; Michael Collins, pilot of the command module *Columbia*; and Edwin E. Aldrin, Jr., pilot of the lunar module *Eagle*.

ALL: NASA

Because the lunar module, which would actually land on the moon, only had to function in airless space and did not have to contend with the earth's atmosphere, engineers were free to design the first nonstreamlined flying vehicle. The result was an ungainly but efficient contraption once described as "a stack of hatboxes piled precariously on top of four spindly legs." The $2,000,000,000 LM, a combination rocket and spacecraft, had been tested in two previous manned missions but had never actually landed anywhere until the Apollo XI flight. Below, Collins, alone in the command ship *Columbia,* photographed the LM on the way to its first touchdown with Armstrong and Aldrin aboard.

MEN ON THE MOON

ALL: NASA

At 4:17 P.M. (E.D.T.), Neil Armstrong radioed to earth. "Houston. Tranquility Base here—the *Eagle* has landed." Man was on the moon! But history was just beginning to be made. At 10:56 P.M., Armstrong emerged from the LM and became the first man to stand on a celestial body other than the earth. "That's one small step for a man, one giant leap for mankind," he said as he touched the moon's surface. Eighteen minutes later, he photographed Edwin Aldrin (left) backing down the LM's steps. Above, Armstrong, taking another picture, is reflected in Aldrin's visor.

Apollo XI casts its shadow over the southwest section of the moon's Sea of Tranquility. When this photograph was taken, both *Eagle* and *Columbia* were still docked and in a lunar orbit.

HERE MEN FROM THE PLANET EARTH
FIRST SET FOOT UPON THE MOON
JULY 1969, A. D.
WE CAME IN PEACE FOR ALL MANKIND

NEIL A. ARMSTRONG
ASTRONAUT

MICHAEL COLLINS
ASTRONAUT

EDWIN E. ALDRIN, JR.
ASTRONAUT

RICHARD NIXON
PRESIDENT, UNITED STATES OF AMERICA

EXPLORING THE UNKNOWN

One of Neil Armstrong's first tasks on the moon was the planting of a specially constructed U.S. flag. intended, according to .the wording of an act of Congress, as a "symbolic gesture of national pride" not a "claim of sovereignty." (The astronauts carried many other flags with them, including those of the 50 states and the United Nations.) Also symbolic of the spirit of the mission was the plaque on the opposite page. Attached to a rung of the ladder of the descent stage. it was left behind with the LM to mark the *Eagle*'s landing spot. The astronauts explored the moon for 2 hours and 13 minutes, collecting about 50 pounds of lunar rocks and soil and conducting a number of scientific experiments. Below, Edwin Aldrin is depicted setting in place instruments to detect ground tremors.

ALL: NASA

BENEFITS TO MANKIND

In creating NASA, Congress stipulated that "activities in space should be devoted to peaceful purposes for the benefit of all mankind." Toward that goal, the agency has developed "applications" satellites to facilitate navigation, communications, and weather observations. The communications program began in 1960 with Echo I, a huge aluminum-coated balloon. Far more complex satellites, such as the Relay, had proved so successful that in 1965 the first commercial communications satellite, Early Bird (later Intelsat I), was put into operation. The Intelsat system now forms a complete transatlantic and transpacific network handling every type of communications need. In addition, the Defense Department operates a separate system linking U.S. military forces around the globe. As spectacular as these "first generation" systems seem they are only beginnings; many are already being replaced by satellites that are far more sophisticated and efficient. Meanwhile, although the success of Apollo 11 showed that the United States could put men on the moon and bring them back again safely, many scientists during the early 1970's became critical of NASA's programs, charging that they emphasized technology at the expense of scientific investigation. Moreover, the Russians demonstrated that unmanned robot moon vehicles, like Lunokhod 1, might eventually achieve some of the goals of manned flights at a fraction of their cost and at no risk to human life. For budgetary reasons, Apollo 18, 19, and 20 were cancelled, and NASA announced that the lunar program would terminate with Apollo 17 in December, 1972. At the same time, it said that the program would gradually become more scientifically oriented. The Apollo 12 mission, which landed on the moon in November, 1969, left behind a highly sophisticated array of instruments, including elaborate devices to test the moon's atmosphere and measure its magnetic fields, study particles from the sun, and solve the mystery of the moon's origin and composition. Apollo 12 astronauts made the first color telecast from the moon's surface and demonstrated that a lunar module could be set down on a specific site, thus enabling future exploration of the moon's more rugged regions. Apollo 13, launched in April, 1971, became an epic voyage of survival after a power failure resulted in the termination of its scheduled lunar landing. Between Apollo 14 in February, 1971, which was billed as the first truly scientific mission, and the even more spectacular Apollo 15 mission in July, 1971, occurred the Soyuz 11 tragedy. Three Soviet astronauts, on a prolonged space-station test voyage, died when their ship suddenly lost cabin pressure on its return to earth. As a result, American astronauts aboard Apollo 15 wore their full space suits when they jettisoned the lunar landing craft prior to starting their homeward journey from the moon. This twelve-day expedition to the rugged lunar Apennine Mountains included many innovations, such as the use of the Rover, a jeeplike vehicle that enabled the astronauts to travel extensively on the moon's surface. One of the most promising finds of the Apollo 15 mission was the discovery of a crystalline rock, which became known as the genesis rock because it may be part of the original lunar crust and may provide valuable clues as to how the moon—and maybe even the earth—were formed.

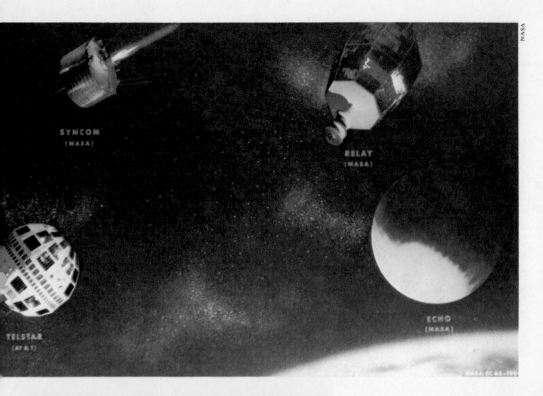

SYNCOM
(NASA)

RELAY
(NASA)

TELSTAR
(AT & T)

ECHO
(NASA)

NASA

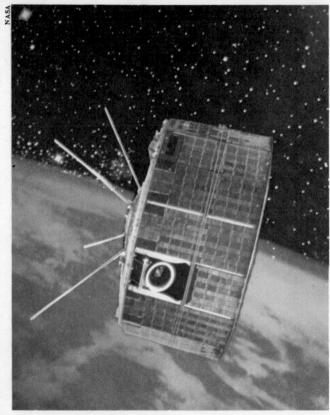

NASA

The composite above represents NASA's early communications effort. While the Echo could only reflect radio signals, the others all had transmitters and receivers. Telstar, the first satellite to be commercially financed, was launched in 1962; among other operations, it tested television and telephone transmissions. NASA's research in weather observation started with Tiros I, a forerunner of the Tiros X at left. Since 1966, a fully operational system, run by the U.S. Weather Bureau and linked to foreign and domestic ground stations, has permitted meteorologists not only to make more accurate forecasts, but also to spot and track violent storms as they are developing.

TO MARS AND BEYOND

Many future plans for space exploration call for flights to Mars in the 1980s. Mariner probes (below) are scheduled for 1971, and "soft" landings from orbiting satellites (above) in 1973. In addition, according to one-time NASA head Thomas O. Paine, a "comfortably appointed orbiting space station," perhaps like the artist's conception at right, may be in use by 1984. "No longer must all of humanity's hopes and fears reside on our shrinking home planet earth," he declared.

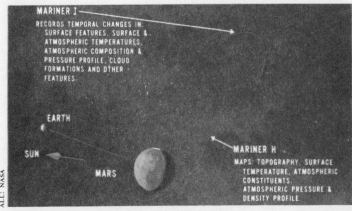

MARINER I
RECORDS TEMPORAL CHANGES IN SURFACE FEATURES, SURFACE & ATMOSPHERIC TEMPERATURES, ATMOSPHERIC COMPOSITION & PRESSURE PROFILE, CLOUD FORMATIONS AND OTHER FEATURES

EARTH

SUN

MARS

MARINER H
MAPS: TOPOGRAPHY, SURFACE TEMPERATURE, ATMOSPHERIC CONSTITUENTS, ATMOSPHERIC PRESSURE & DENSITY PROFILE

ALL: NASA

CHAPTER 47

CONFLICTS AND ACHIEVEMENTS

"The torch has passed to a new generation of Americans— born in this century. . . ." The words, ringing out in the chill Washington air on January 20, 1961, heralded a different kind of Presidency from the grandfatherly Eisenhower years. "Ask not what your country can do for you," Democrat John F. Kennedy demanded, "ask what you can do for your country." Kennedy made it clear that America's youngest President since Theodore Roosevelt would be "in the forefront of the battle," and he called for the involvement of the whole nation in the American enterprise. He inherited an America that had come a long way from the relative simplicities of the immediate postwar years. The technological legacy of two major wars was transforming every

Although John F. Kennedy was President for less than three years, his impact on the nation was enormous. To many he seemed to be the embodiment of revived idealism in American political life.

major sector of life—industrial, commercial, agricultural, and social. Jet transportation forded the oceans of the world faster than the railroads of less than 25 years before had negotiated the routes between the major cities. Communications brought the events and the ideas of the entire world into the living room of the average American, informing his thinking, widening his views. Unlike the post-World War I period when America retreated into isolation, the United States was now a world leader. The nation's unparalleled economic position had much to do with the difference. The gross national product, the total value of all goods and services produced in the United States, had risen from nearly $212,000,000,000 in 1945 to more than $503,000,000,000 in 1960. Median family income stood at $5,835 for whites, $3,233 for non-whites; household savings totaled $72,000,000,000,000; the civilian labor force reached 70,000,000— an increase of 16,000,000 jobs

*The televised Kennedy-Nixon debates in 1960 helped put the lesser-known
Senator before the nation and established a new method of campaigning.*

since the end of the war. The nation
which for more than a century had
celebrated the virtues of the home
and stability had also developed a
wanderlust. Sociologists called it
mobility. It affected jobs—labor stat-
isticians estimated that the typical
American breadwinner would change
employers no less than seven times
during his work life. It affected home
life also—approximately 1,000,000
families a year were picking up
stakes and decamping to new parts
of the country and countryside.

However, if the average American
felt free to pursue his prosperous
dream of a home in the suburbs,
there was another American who
could not. He went by many names.
He was disadvantaged, with little

schooling and few skills. He was
numbered among the 6% of the work
force that was unemployed. He was
the urban poor, nesting among the
rotting tenements of the big-city
black ghettoes. He was the semi-
skilled agricultural worker, dis-
placed by farm mechanization. He
was the migrant laborer, never settling long enough in one place to
get his family established and his
children educated. He was the low-
skilled industrial worker bumped by
automation. "One third of all
Americans go to bed hungry each
night," Kennedy had charged in his
campaign against Vice-President
Richard M. Nixon. "We must do
better." Although the statistic was
overdrawn in campaign rhetoric, the

condition was not. Henceforth, the attack upon both urban and rural poverty would receive priority among the nation's objectives.

Kennedy went on to defeat Nixon by the slim margin of 117,574 popular votes out of nearly 69,000,000 cast, though his electoral tally was a comfortable 303 to Nixon's 219.

In his inaugural, the new President depicted the cause of freedom as being in its hour of "maximum peril," and, mixing both domestic and foreign-policy goals, asked for the nation's support in "a struggle against the common enemies of man: tyranny, poverty, disease and war itself." This struggle was almost immediately focused on American-Soviet relations. Kennedy was persuaded that Russia had a temporary lead over the United States in weapons technology, particularly in the development of nuclear-delivery systems. The so-called missile gap had been one of his favorite themes during the campaign. There was, moreover, ample reason to credit the Russians with a highly developed capacity in rocketry. They had shocked the thinly financed American space establishment in the geophysical year of 1957 with the successful launching of Sputnik I, the first earth satellite. As a result, the United States had belatedly switched from special scientific rockets to military rockets for satellite exploration of near space, but the U.S.S.R. continued to reap prestige from an impressive array of "firsts."

Unrest in Russia

Despite the policy of "peaceful coexistence" enunciated by Soviet chairman Khrushchev, relations between the two superpowers in 1961 were at their lowest ebb since the Stalin era. In May of the previous year, after an American U-2 spy plane had been downed inside the Soviet Union, Khrushchev had broken up a summit conference in Paris by loudly denouncing an infuriated President Eisenhower. Evidence has since accumulated that Khrushchev was acting under extreme internal pressure. He had decided in 1954 to increase the number of acres under cultivation instead of building more fertilizer plants. The so-called virgin lands program was designed to put Soviet agriculture on an independent footing. However, by 1957, Khrushchev's agricultural policy had been defeated by the short growing season on the Russian Steppes. His determination to build a Russian consumer society was also facing stiff opposition from those within the government who wanted to continue to build up heavy industry and export production. The spy-plane incident and the show trial of the captured pilot, Francis Gary Powers, was a tailor-made diversion for Khrushchev, whose political status at home seemed to depend upon keeping international tensions at a high pitch.

Kennedy set out to reduce these tensions by gathering the loose strands of the diplomatic dialogue between the two countries, but his first year in office was a dismal one for American foreign policy. On April 12, 1961, Russia's prestige

Fidel Castro's speeches spellbound the Cubans after he came to power. But he himself was soon spellbound by Russia.

as a leading technological nation was impressively advanced with the world's first manned space orbit by Soviet Air Force Major Yuri Gagarin. Five days later, the international prestige of the United States plummeted when an American-organized and financed invasion of Cuba by anti-Communist exiles failed on the beaches of the Bay of Pigs. On June 3 and 4, the President met with Khrushchev in Vienna for a hastily arranged summit conference. He came away shocked by the Soviet leader's intransigence. In an effort to convince the Russians that America was determined to support its European allies, the following month Kennedy countered a Communist proposal to make Berlin into a demilitarized "free city" by saying he would increase the size of U.S. military forces. On August 13, East Germany closed the border between East and West Berlin—first with barbed wire, then with an eight-foot-high masonry wall—to stop the flight of East Berliners to the more prosperous Western sector. Russia then began rattling her thermonuclear arsenal, setting off several hydrogen test blasts in October to demonstrate her might. The following year, Khrushchev made an offensive thrust into the Western Hemisphere that brought about the most dangerous face-off of the cold war.

Since the abortive invasion attempt at the Bay of Pigs, Russia had

When the Soviet Union removed her missiles from Cuba in 1962, an American warship (foreground) steamed alongside to inspect the cargo on deck.

been arming Cuba. The United States took the position that so long as the arms buildup on the Communist island remained defensive, there would be no interference. However, by mid-October of 1962 evidence began to accumulate that Russia was installing intermediate-range missiles in Fidel Castro's Cuba. Kennedy's response was swift. At the United Nations, U.S. Ambassador Adlai E. Stevenson presented the photographic documentation of new medium-range missile sites and dramatically challenged the Soviet ambassador to deny it. On the mili-

tary front, Kennedy put into effect a naval "quarantine" of Cuba—a selective blockade authorized to stop, search, and turn back any vessels carrying missiles. On the night of October 22, Kennedy informed the American public of his stand, and the world held its breath. The two superpowers stood like barroom fighters, "eyeball to eyeball." As a fleet of Communist merchant vessels carrying missiles on their open decks approached Cuban waters, communications between Washington and Moscow began to carry messages from the Soviet leadership, at first denying offensive intentions in Cuba but finally agreeing to turn back the fleet. Washington made the further demand that the missiles already in Cuba be pulled out. With appropriate face-saving language, the Soviets agreed. The crisis was over.

The showdown actually resulted in more realistic relations between the two countries. The United States had demonstrated that it would not tolerate an open threat to its territory. Russia, in effect, admitted that she had pushed too hard, and she backed off. The nature of the American military response was such that Russia could do so with some grace, and it was this carefully calculated initiative that probably saved the day. Both nations, thoroughly shaken by the close call, almost immediately reopened negotiations on a limited nuclear-test ban, and a "hot line" was installed between the White House and the Kremlin to permit instantaneous communication in times of crisis. Within a year, the United States and Russia had worked out a pact to halt all testing in the atmosphere, under the seas, and in outer space. More than 100 other nations signed the treaty in October, 1963. France, intent on developing her own nuclear strike capacity, refused to sign, as did Red China. Nevertheless, the treaty was a substantial step toward limiting the spread of nuclear potential. Inasmuch as the ban involved coop-

erative effort, it was also a step toward the easing of international tensions. Other tentative steps were being taken. Trade barriers with a number of the nations in Eastern Europe—first Marshal Tito's independently minded Yugoslavia, then others—were being bridged. The United States, for the first time since the war, was selling wheat directly to Russia. Cultural exchanges were being arranged, and a new mood of international understanding was prevalent.

Civil rights as an issue

Meanwhile, the strings of domestic crisis were growing taut. Presented daily with the evidence of growing affluence, the black American was becoming impatient with the slowly grinding wheels of economic and social justice. Steps to correct unequal treatment of racial minorities had been in progress ever since the war. This progress was admittedly slow. In 1948, Truman by executive order outlawed racial segregation in the armed forces. The Federal Housing Act of 1949 forbade racial discrimination in federally financed housing. In the landmark case of *Brown vs. Board of Education of Topeka, Kansas* in 1954, the Supreme Court struck down the 58-year-old doctrine of "separate but equal" accommodations for white and black schoolchildren and ordered Southern school districts to integrate their classes. The federal

Earl Warren (seated, center) becomes a symbol of constitutional liberalism as Chief Justice. Above is the "Warren Court" as it looked after 1962.

courts later extended this doctrine to the Northern states, where, it was successfully argued, the concept of the neighborhood school district resulted in de facto segregation. The White House, Eisenhower made clear, was prepared to back the court's decisions with direct action.

In 1957, pursuant to the Supreme Court decision the Little Rock, Arkansas, board of education adopted a plan of integration that called for the admission of some Negroes to the city's Central High School, starting in September. As the time for the opening of school approached, Governor Orval E. Faubus declared that integration would threaten the peace. He then stationed national guard units around the high school. When nine Negroes attempted to enroll, Faubus ordered the national guard to keep them from enrolling.

Under federal injunction, the national guard was withdrawn. Then rioting mobs appeared, bent on keeping Negroes from the school. At that juncture, Eisenhower ordered 1,000 federal paratroopers into the city and pressed the national guard into federal service, thereby removing it from the governor's control. Under the protection of federal bayonets, the Negroes entered the school. Thus, the principle that the federal government would not tolerate any local defiance of court orders on integration was established.

There were some federal actions in behalf of civil rights besides those taken by the courts. In 1957, Congress passed the Civil Rights Act,

In 1965, Martin Luther King led 25,000 marchers from Selma to Montgomery, Alabama. Ralph Bunche is on Dr. King's right; Mrs. King is on his left.

the first significant legislation in the field since Reconstruction. It created a federal Civil Rights Commission and gave the government new power to seek injunctions against interference with Negro voting.

Much of the impetus toward faster desegregation, however, came from the Negroes themselves, together with some supporting whites. In 1960, a group of Negro students entered a department store in Greensboro, North Carolina, and sat quietly at the lunch counter to protest the fact that Negroes were not served there. This was the beginning of the "sit-in" movement that spread quickly through the South and resulted in the desegregation of several lunch counters and public waiting rooms. A year later, some Negro organizations started the practice of "freedom rides"—Negroes and whites riding through the South and entering "white" waiting rooms. Many of the sit-in demonstrators and freedom riders were arrested, and some were attacked; but they succeeded in quickening the pace of desegregation.

As the pace quickened, resistance in many parts of the country stiffened. In 1962–63, the governors of both Alabama and Mississippi attempted to prevent Negroes from enrolling in their respective state universities. As a result, national guard troops, activated by President Kennedy, had to be employed to quell violent riots. In Birmingham, Alabama, a protest march led by the Reverend Dr. Martin Luther King, Jr., was interrupted by Police Commissioner Eugene "Bull" Connor, who unleashed a pack of police dogs on the marchers and jailed Dr. King. A church in Birmingham was bombed, killing and maiming Negro children. On the very night that President Kennedy, in a televised speech, called for a settlement of the "moral issue" racial injustice had become, Medgar Evers, Mississippi chief of the National Association for the Advancement of Colored People, was assassinated in Jackson.

On June 19, 1963, Kennedy sent the strongest civil-rights bill in history to Congress. The bill called for a public-accommodations section, which would make it illegal to discriminate in public facilities, granted the Attorney General authority to file suit where school desegregation had not been carried out, assured

Lincoln Memorial was the focal point for blacks and whites at the well-attended civil-rights Freedom March on Washington on August 28, 1963.

fair employment and voter-registration practices, and withheld federal funds from projects in which discrimination was practiced. When it became apparent that Congressional action was not going to be as swift as had been hoped, Negro leaders announced plans for a march on Washington. Kennedy was apprehensive. If fewer than the estimated 100,000 marchers should show up, he reasoned, Congress might feel that passage of the bill was not urgent.

However, on August 28, 1963, more than 250,000 black and white Americans converged on Washington and heard Dr. King describe his dream "that one day on the red hills of Georgia the sons of former slaves and the sons of former slave-owners will be able to sit down together at the table of brotherhood."

The President is slain

Then, abruptly, the unthinkable occurred. President John F. Kennedy was fatally shot in Dallas, Texas, on November 22, 1963. Not since McKinley's death in 1901 had an American President been assassinated. Kennedy, whose identification with civil-rights causes had made him a target of right-wing extremism and Southern conservatism, had been mending political fences in the key state of Texas. Paradoxically, he was slain by a young left-wing fanatic, Lee Harvey Oswald. Oswald was arrested that afternoon and two days later was himself fatally shot by a Dallas nightclub owner, Jack Ruby, while being escorted through a corridor by Dallas policemen. The shock waves spread around the world. Kennedy had made of the young and youthful his special constituency. Not only young people, but also young nations identified their interests with his, and his Presidency had done much to restore a sense of the nation's ideals both at home and abroad. By the thousands, the young had rushed to join his 1961 creation, the Peace Corps, a cadre of technicians, teachers, and professional men and women that was set up to aid developing nations.

By the millions, young and old alike mourned him around the world. America rallied to bury its murdered President with ceremonies of dignity and honor, and efficiently transferred power to the new President, Lyndon B. Johnson. As Johnson told Congress, "This is our challenge—not to hesitate, not to pause, not to turn about and linger over this evil moment but to continue on our course so that we may fulfill the destiny that history has set for us."

Johnson entered the White House aware that he would not fall undisputed heir to the loyalty Kennedy

John F. Kennedy was the fourth American President to be killed by an assassin's bullet. While the world wept, his coffin lay in state in the Capitol Rotunda.

commanded from the powerful liberal wing of the Democratic Party. Yet he needed this loyalty if he were to reanimate the old Democratic coalition originally constructed by his Presidential model, Franklin D. Roosevelt. Both Kennedy and Johnson had sensed in 1960 that the nation needed new goals. Kennedy spoke to this need in 1961 when he set the space program on its course to the moon. Both addressed themselves to it in their many expressions on the quality of American life and the gaps that had opened between the comfortable majority and the deprived minorities. Johnson would need the whole of his party behind him if he were to be effective in setting the nation upon a new course. He therefore determined first to push Kennedy's domestic program through Congress.

The Johnson approach

One of the most experienced politicians ever to reach the Presidency, Johnson was an altogether different sort of man from Kennedy. He was an expert in the arts of manipulation and bargaining. Combining his own skills with the willingness of most Congressmen to build a legislative memorial to Kennedy, Johnson energetically engineered a spectacular series of legislative successes. The Civil Rights Act of 1964, which had been languishing in committee since Kennedy's proposal, and a tax cut—to name the most

significant of many achievements—were quickly enacted into law during Johnson's first year in office.

Despite his many years of public service, Johnson entered the Presidency as an unknown quantity. While his record in Congress had been generally conservative, he had, as Vice-President, worked tirelessly to advance the liberal causes of the Kennedy administration. As President, however, he announced that he would seek a national consensus, that he intended to be President of all the people. He began by declaring war on poverty in America.

Built around the Office of Economic Opportunity, Johnson's anti-poverty measures provided for, among other things, a domestic peace corps known as VISTA (Volunteers in Service to America), a Job Corps for teaching vocational skills to disadvantaged young Americans, a Neighborhood Youth Corps to reach and convert to useful activities the street gangs of the big cities, plus a number of other assistance measures for farmers, migrant workers, small businessmen, and undereducated adults. Later, a Model Cities program was added to provide tangible examples of urban residential reconstruction. The legislative performance was truly remarkable. Johnson had wrung from a Congress that was as reluctant as those that had blocked the domestic programs of two prior Democratic Presidents, a summary expression of unprecedented national goals: end poverty, eliminate racial, economic, and educational discrimination, halt urban decay—now!

These remarkable goals proved easier to express in law than to accomplish in fact. From the start, with rare exception the new poverty programs ran into constant administrative and executive problems. Sectional and local resistance exploited the difficulties, and Americans began to wonder about Johnson's bright vision of "The Great Society."

Yet as America moved into the election year of 1964, the Johnson administration—its legislative successes still largely untarnished—was clearly in the ascendant. With the exception of the Deep South, his party had not appeared more unified since the Roosevelt era. Johnson's nomination was only a formality. The Republicans nominated Arizona Senator Barry M. Goldwater, a conservative. The Democrats immediately set out to show that Goldwater was even more conservative than his own party believed him to be, and the G.O.P. candidate did little to combat this impression. It was Goldwater's belief that the millions of Americans who did not vote in Presidential elections—sometimes as much as 40% of the electorate—abstained because both parties in recent years had chosen liberal candidates for the Presidency. Goldwater hoped to entice this silent

WIDE WORLD

Vice-President Humphrey and President Johnson together at the White House.

vote into a new coalition. He saw the nation facing two clear ideological choices—left or right—and he was determined to offer his candidacy as "a choice, not an echo."

Johnson, however, refused to follow Goldwater's scenario. He believed that the typical American would identify with moderate sentiments. The President's choice of the middle ground frustrated the Republican campaign strategists. Presented with a Republican candidate effectively depicted as "extreme," the American voters

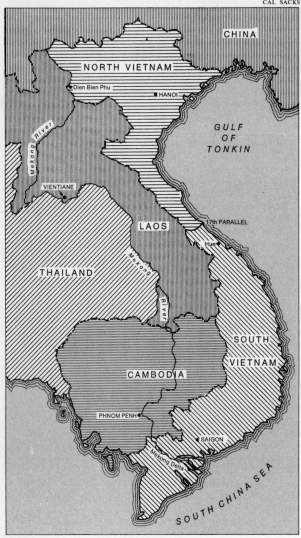

South Vietnam's fate was considered vital to all Indochina when war erupted.

went to the polls and proved Johnson's assessment of the public mind overwhelmingly correct. He won the Presidency in his own right with 486 electoral votes to Goldwater's 52. In the process, his party strengthened its hold on the Congress by one seat in the Senate and 37 in the House. A President so mandated and so endowed might have looked forward to a term of high accomplishment. But an Asian booby trap awaited Lyndon Baines Johnson.

Escalation of the war

American involvement in the Vietnam war had been building steadily under three Presidents. From a small advisory force numbering in the hundreds originally authorized in 1954 by President Eisenhower, the size and the scope of American military commitments had steadily grown. By 1963, there were more than 15,500 U.S. troops in Vietnam, making command decisions in the field, flying air-support missions, and providing fire support and reconnaissance at sea. This commitment was to expand radically under Johnson. In August, 1964, torpedo boats from North Vietnam attacked two American destroyers in the Gulf of Tonkin. Within a week of the incident, Johnson had secured from the Congress a joint resolution authorizing him to "take all necessary measures" to repel armed attacks against American forces in Vietnam and, more important, "to prevent further aggression." This amounted practically to a military carte blanche. The authorization was used gingerly at first. Gradually, however, it was extended to cover not only retaliatory raids upon northern military installations but also strategic bombing of the North Vietnamese industrial war machine and transportation network. By February, 1965, air sorties against North Vietnam had become routine.

Four months later, after the appearance of North Vietnamese regulars on South Vietnamese soil, American troops now numbering some 50,000 men were shifted from advisory to combat status.

As Vietnam became more and more an American enterprise, the United States pressed repeatedly on the diplomatic front for negotiations that might end the conflict. On the war front, the Johnson administration engaged in a kind of carrot-and-stick strategy. Repeatedly the President ordered periodic halts to the bombing raids on the North, while peace feelers were put out.

With each rebuff, the war effort escalated. Two years after the Tonkin Gulf incident, U.S. forces were in excess of 350,000, and war deaths had risen to more than 6,500.

By 1967, the Vietnamese war had become the single most important issue in the country, and its drain upon the country's human and economic resources had eroded President Johnson's consensus. The first mechanism of consensus to fail was the President's wage-price guidelines. Under the guidelines, there had been tacit but substantial agreement among government, labor, and management that prices of basic

United States Marines search for Vietcong in a marsh in South Vietnam. Nearly 550,000 American servicemen were stationed in that divided country by the spring of 1968.

President Lyndon Johnson and Soviet Premier Aleksei Kosygin confer in Glassboro, New Jersey, in June, 1967. Their meeting was helpful, but produced no concrete results.

commodities would be held relatively stable and that wage increases would be kept close to the estimated annual rise of worker productivity—roughly 3%. Basic steel prices led the guideline breakdown. They rose to $14 a ton. A series of wage increases ranging up to 8% soon followed, and inflation, creeping along at a relatively stable 2% annually, broke into a gallop. The consumer price index indicated a 4% price rise in 1967, and by that summer Johnson was forced to ask Congress for a

10% income-tax surcharge to dampen the inflationary surge and to cover the mounting costs of the Vietnam conflict. Meanwhile, the antiwar sentiment in Congress grew louder. Senator J. William Fulbright (Democrat, Arkansas), chairman of the Senate Foreign Relations Committee, questioned Johnson's broad interpretation of the Tonkin Gulf Resolution. Senator Robert F. Kennedy (Democrat, New York), the late President's brother, called for a halt in the bombing of North Vietnam, and sentiment began to arise in the black community that the war was siphoning away resources vital to the antipoverty effort.

In June, 1967, President Johnson, seeking still another avenue to peace, met with Premier Aleksei Kosygin of the Soviet Union at Glassboro State College in New Jersey. Russia was supplying the North Vietnamese, and it was hoped that she could use her influence to bring the Hanoi government to the conference table. Russia, however, was engaged in an ideological war with Communist China. Any overt efforts on her part to help with the peace effort would be immediately poisoned by Chinese propaganda.

In addition, the worldwide competition between the two superpowers had found another explosive outlet in the Middle East, where Arab power centered in President Gamal Abdel Nasser's Egypt confronted the small but highly developed state of Israel. Nasser had sought to rally the Arab world behind him since his rise to power in the early 1950s by making both a religious and territorial issue of Israel. An uneasy truce, supervised by the United Nations, had prevailed for more than a decade. However,

Nasser, now lavishly equipped by the Soviets, felt he was ready. In May, gathering Syria and Jordan to his cause, Nasser occuped the disputed Gaza Strip on the Mediterranean coast, closed the Gulf of Aqaba east of Suez to Israeli shipping, and ordered the U.N. truce force to leave the area. Israel, in a lightning display of military power, destroyed the Egyptian air force, retook the Gaza Strip, occupied the Jordanian half of Jerusalem, as well as the strategic Golan Heights, and drove through the Sinai Peninsula to the Suez Canal. Both the United States and the Soviet Union took steps to reassure each other they would not intervene while their surrogates battled. However, the war was over in six days, and to the

Anti-American demonstrations have occurred often in both friendly and unfriendly countries. Here, the Chinese Red Guards attack U.S. "imperialism."

acute embarrassment of the Russians the Egyptian fighting potential lay strewn in ruins around Israel's widened borders.

As America entered the election year of 1968, the Vietnam effort was costing in the neighborhood of $25,000,000,000 a year. Inflationary pressures were increasing. War deaths had risen past 15,000, and troop commitments stood at more than 475,000—more men than America had sent to Korea at the height of that conflict. Military assurances that the United States was winning were seriously undermined on January 30, when the Communists launched an offensive against the major cities of South Vietnam during Tet, the lunar New Year. They shattered Saigon, and for five days occupied the northern provincial capital of Hue. The Johnson administration's reaction was both to raise troop commitments to nearly 550,000 and to press efforts to hold peace talks.

On March 31, President Johnson announced the unilateral cessation of bombing missions over 90% of North Vietnam. He called upon Hanoi to respond to this new initiative. Then, dramatically, he relieved the gesture of any subsequent suggestion that his move was prompted by election-year political motives: "I shall not seek, and I will not accept the nomination of my party for another term as your President." Johnson, in short, had sacrificed his remarkable political career in an all-out gamble to bring Hanoi to the conference table. At last the Communists responded, and negotiations between North Vietnam and the United States were arranged. Talks opened in Paris on May 10, but the heavy toll of the war hardly abated. The Tet offensive and a follow-up series of attacks in May had proved costly to the Communists. Nevertheless, the attacks had also brought American battle deaths since 1961 to more than 25,000.

The crises at home

The war had also worked its evils at home, contributing to a mounting debate over the nation's moral values and creating what many believed was an obstacle to solving increasing domestic divisions. Black communities in cities across the nation had revolted violently in the summer of 1967, and the President's Commission on Civil Disorder early in 1968 reported pointedly that closing the gap between the expectations of the poor and their present condition required the nation's highest priority. Militancy among college students—supporting the civil-rights movement, dissenting from the war, and, on the far left, revolting against the whole value structure they labeled the Establishment—widened the so-called generation gap.

Within the broad middle ground of the American political spectrum, corrosive forces were also at work.

Inflation, the human sacrifice of the war, student alienation, and the economic and emotional anxieties generated by the numerous ailments called the urban crisis, all combined to raise grave questions about the quality of American leadership and the effectiveness of the nation's social and governmental institutions. Thus beset, an America in conflict, both inside and outside its borders, was asked to choose a President.

Their choice was Richard M. Nixon. He took office on January 20, 1969, with an uncertain mandate. In a three-way race with Vice-President Hubert H. Humphrey and former Alabama Governor George C. Wallace, Nixon attracted less than 43.4% of the popular vote. In a very real sense, the election results reflected the national mood, depressed and divided by a year of almost unprecedented political and civil strife on the domestic front and by unrelieved frustration abroad. The seizure of the American intelligence ship, U.S.S. *Pueblo*, in the Sea of Japan on January 23, 1968, by the North Koreans exposed once more the powerlessness of the nation to deal decisively with small belligerent powers in a nuclear age. The continuing failure of the Paris Peace

In the mid-1960s, Negro frustrations turned into violence. Scores of cities, such as Detroit above in July, 1967, turned into riot-torn battlefields.

Conference to bring any measurable reduction in the level of the Vietnam ground fighting added its contribution to expanding doubts about foreign and military policy.

At home, frustration with the war and the growing racial strife in the cities found explosive and often perverse expression throughout the year. The assassinations of Dr. Martin Luther King, Jr., leader of the nonviolent wing of the black man's quest for equality, in April, and of Robert Kennedy less than two months later were perhaps the most tragic symptoms of what many called "a national malaise."

This divisive spirit found political tongue. The Democrats were the first to split. Senator Eugene J. McCarthy (Democrat, Minnesota), in attacking the Vietnam war on moral and practical grounds, gathered a corps of young adherents to his Presidential candidacy and stunned Johnson and his party by polling 42.2% of the Democratic vote in the New Hampshire primary election in March. It was the same month that Johnson announced he would not seek another term and Robert Kennedy entered the race.

Wallace, running with retired Air Force General Curtis LeMay, pressed his third-party candidacy beyond the borders of Dixie, in an effort to link Southern conservatism with Northern middle-class unrest over the racial issue and urban crime. The simple words

Richard M. Nixon and Spiro T. Agnew triumphed for the Republicans in 1968.

"law and order" took on an anti-black bias, and Americans found they could no longer count upon a common language. Slogans meant different things, not only from region to region but from neighborhood to neighborhood.

The Democratic Convention in Chicago further divided the party when antiwar demonstrators collided violently with Chicago police as network television cameras looked on. In Miami, the Republicans quietly picked Nixon and Maryland Governor Spiro T. Agnew. The summer ended and, almost miraculously, the cities had escaped a repetition of the racial violence of the year before.

In the campaign, the candidates of the two major parties—both of them experienced and astute in the arts of elective politics—sought to rally the crumbling middle ground, that elusive center of the American political system. Each approached the task from a different direction. Humphrey, burdened with the Johnson administration's war policy and the riotous debacle of the Chicago convention, pinned his strategic hopes on a coalition of big-city election machinery, the black vote, the progressive traditions of labor, and the moderate sentiments of the middle class. The Southern conservative vote was lost, in his view, preferably to Wallace.

Nixon, on the other hand, approached the middle seeking to draw the moderately conservative border states, the farm vote, and the suburbs of the major cities into a new coalition. He viewed this coalition as committed to an orderly settlement of the Vietnam issue and a compromise of the traditional conflict between property rights and individual rights in the struggle for racial equality. He was successful—but barely. The Nixon-Agnew team lost every major city in the nation, but captured such key states as California, Illinois, and Indiana to win an electoral majority of 301 votes in 32 states. Humphrey and his running mate, Senator Edmund

S. Muskie (Democrat, Maine), took 191 electoral votes in 13 states and the District of Columbia. The Wallace strategy failed to carry a single Northern or border state. He did, however, capture Alabama, Arkansas, Georgia, Louisiana, and Mississippi, with their 46 electoral votes. Moreover, his 10,151,000 popular votes were the most in history for a third-party candidate.

The Nixon administration

The nation's 37th President entered office determined to haul the Presidency out of the vortex of daily crisis and carry it to higher, quieter ground, where the nation's problems could be viewed in perspective and solved at some remove from the heat of the controversy. "Let us lower our voices," Nixon implored his fellow Americans in his inaugural. "Watch what we do, not what we say," suggested one cabinet officer.

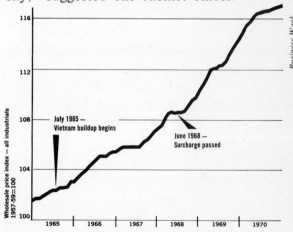

The rise in wholesale prices mirrors the inflation that accompanied escalation of U.S. military involvement in Vietnam.

The slaying of four antiwar Kent State students by Ohio National Guardsmen on May 4, 1970, touched off campus protests throughout the nation.

Political observers did watch, searching for indications of which way Nixon would head. But the clues were sparse at first, for the new President moved with caution. Unlike his predecessors, who had been forced by circumstances to decide domestic or foreign issues of great moment within their first hundred days in office, Nixon took his time in assembling his cabinet and measuring his actions until it became clear, at least at first, that his intention was to maintain a middle course, especially with regard to the two major issues that he faced from the outset—the war in Vietnam and a declining economy.

Nixon's war policy

The President stated that he had no intention of prosecuting the war to its fullest extent. Similarly, he ruled out an immediate and total withdrawal of all American combat troops from Vietnam. Following the lead already taken by Lyndon Johnson, he resolved to seek a negotiated peace. Partly in response to mounting anti-war protests at home and partly to revive stalled preliminary peace talks in Paris, he initiated a gradual withdrawal of United States forces in June, 1969. According to his timetable, nearly half of the 550,000 Americans serving in Vietnam were to be brought home by the spring of 1971.

Crucial to this pullback was the gradual takeover of American combat duties by South Vietnamese forces. But the President was concerned that the American withdrawal would merely serve to delay new enemy attacks until American forces were no longer on hand to bolster South Vietnamese troops. Accordingly, in late April, 1970, after he was advised of an enemy buildup in neighboring Cambodia, the President ordered an American offensive into that country. Its purpose, he said, was to destroy "the headquarters for the entire Communist military operation in South Vietnam." Once enemy forces were driven out of their staging and supply sanctuaries in Cambodia, he said, "we will withdraw." Nixon described the offensive as a necessary extension of the war, designed to save American lives in the long run and shorten the war.

The Cambodian incursion stimulated the anti-war movement in the United States to its greatest activity.

After long and acrimonious debate, Congress approved a measure that September prohibiting the President from spending further funds without congressional approval to "retain" American forces or military advisers in Cambodia.

In the long run, however, Nixon's

A littered highway symbolizes a growing concern to many people—pollution and other menaces to the earth's ecology.

1415

explanation for ordering the Cambodian invasion, as well as his obvious determination to scale down American participation in the war by withdrawing troops, served to mollify the public. A subsequent measure, which would have required the withdrawal of all American forces from Indochina by the end of 1971, was rejected by the Senate. And when South Vietnamese troops —with American air support—invaded Laos in the winter of 1971, in another move against enemy supply routes, critical reaction was limited.

At the time of the Laos invasion, American fighting strength was down to about 330,000 men, and additional reductions were being planned. At that point, more than 44,000 Americans had been killed in action and nearly 300,000 wounded; South Vietnamese battle deaths totaled nearly 120,000; and, according to American figures, enemy casualties stood at 700,000.

On the home front

The cost of the Vietnam war continued to be felt at home despite the gradual reduction of America's commitment. Inflation and high unemployment became Nixon's other major concern. Prices and wages rose, and the value of the dollar decreased.

In order to pump more federal money into the slumping economy, the President abandoned the idea of a balanced budget and returned the federal government to deficit financing. In addition, in August, 1971, Nixon ordered a nationwide wage-price freeze in order to halt further inflation, and took decisive steps to bolster American manufacturers against foreign competitors.

By mid-term, the President had yet to compile an impressive record of legislative action. However, after weathering the first mail strike in history, he was able to press through establishment of an independent postal service. Also, with his backing, Congress voted to allow 18-year-olds to vote in federal elections and passed a constitutional amendment to lower the minimum voting age in state and local elections, too. In addition, his announcement in mid-July of 1971 that he would visit Communist China, thus affecting a dramatic turn-around in American policy after more than twenty years of enforced isolation, was considered a diplomatic coup. (Nixon also sought to seat Communist China in the U.N., along with Nationalist China; U.N. members approved the seating of the mainland Chinese, but expelled the Taiwan government.)

It seemed clear by late 1971 that the President would seek reelection on the record of what he would ultimately achieve on the two issues that headed his agenda from the start—the war and the economy.

Volume 16
ENCYCLOPEDIC
SECTION

The two-page reference guide below lists the entries by categories. The entries in this section supplement the subject matter covered in the text of this volume. A **cross-reference** (*see*) means that a separate entry appears elsewhere in this section. However, certain important persons and events mentioned here have individual entries in the Encyclopedic Sections of other volumes. Consult the Index in this Volume.

AMERICAN STATESMEN AND POLITICIANS

Dean Acheson

Spiro T. Agnew

Ralph Bunche

Thomas E. Dewey

Everett M. Dirksen

William O. Douglas

John Foster Dulles

Dwight D. Eisenhower

Abe Fortas

J. William Fulbright

Arthur J. Goldberg

Barry Goldwater

Alger Hiss

J. Edgar Hoover

Hubert H. Humphrey

Lyndon B. Johnson

Edward M. Kennedy

John F. Kennedy

Robert F. Kennedy

Eugene J. McCarthy

Joseph R. McCarthy

Thurgood Marshall

Edmund S. Muskie

Richard M. Nixon

Samuel T. Rayburn

Dean Rusk

Adlai E. Stevenson

Robert A. Taft

Harry S. Truman

George C. Wallace

Earl Warren

THE CIVIL-RIGHTS MOVEMENT

Mary McLeod Bethune

Brown vs. Board of Education

Ralph Bunche

Civil Rights Act of 1964

Civil-rights Movement

Martin Luther King, Jr.

Malcolm X

Thurgood Marshall

Jackie Robinson

Voting Rights Act of 1965

THE COLD WAR

Bay of Pigs invasion

Berlin airlift

Gulf of Tonkin resolution

Alger Hiss

Marshall Plan

North Atlantic Treaty Organization

J. Robert Oppenheimer

Pentagon Papers

Pueblo incident

Hyman Rickover

Rosenberg spy case

Southeast Asia Treaty Organization

Truman Doctrine

LABOR

George Meany

Walter Reuther

Taft-Hartley Act

POETS

Robert Frost

Carl Sandburg

THE PRESIDENCY

Dwight D. Eisenhower

Lyndon B. Johnson

John F. Kennedy

Richard M. Nixon

Lee Harvey Oswald

Jack Ruby

Sirhan Sirhan

Harry S. Truman

A

ACHESON, Dean Gooderham
(1893-1971). As Secretary of
State (1949–1953) under President **Harry S. Truman** (*see*),
Acheson helped develop and
implement a policy of containment to prevent Communist expansion by extending American
economic and military aid to
foreign nations. Born in Connecticut, Acheson graduated from
Yale University in 1915. He
subsequently entered Harvard
University Law School, but
interrupted his studies there to
serve as an ensign in the navy
during World War I. He received
his law degree in 1918 and spent
the next two years as private
secretary to Supreme Court
Justice Louis D. Brandeis (1856–
1941). From 1921 to 1933,
Acheson practiced law in Washington D.C. In 1933, President
Franklin D. Roosevelt (1882–
1945) appointed him Undersecretary of the Treasury, but
he resigned the following November because he opposed the
President's plan to raise prices
by devaluating the international
gold rate. Returning to his law
practice, Acheson also headed a
committee engaged in a study of
the federal government's administrative bureaus in 1939–40. In
1940, he became an active member of the Committee to Defend
America by Aiding the Allies, an
organization that opposed a negotiated peace with Germany and
advocated full-scale aid to Britain. These activities led to
Acheson's appointment as Assistant Secretary of State in
1941, a position he held until
1945. He was instrumental in
the passage of the Lend-Lease
Act and subsequently helped to
administer the aid program. He
also played a significant role in
planning the United Nations and
in promoting the United Nations

Dean Acheson

Relief and Rehabilitation Administration, which was established in 1943. While serving as
Undersecretary of State from
1945 to 1947, Acheson was
chairman of a committee to plan
for the international control of
atomic energy. With the intensification of the cold war with the
Soviet Union after 1946. Acheson shifted from a conciliatory
position and became an ardent
champion of containment. In
a speech before Congress in
March, 1947, he explained the
Truman Doctrine (*see*), which
proposed that the United States
aid Greece and Turkey to prevent Communist take-overs in
those countries. Acheson resigned in June, 1947, and practiced law until Truman appointed
him Secretary of State in January, 1949. In Europe, he was
active in implementing the Marshall Plan and also played a
major role in establishing the
North Atlantic Treaty Organization (*see*). In Asian affairs, Acheson attempted to dissociate the
United States from the Nationalist Chinese regime on Formosa

(Taiwan), a policy that was criticized by Democrats as well as
Republicans in Congress. He was
also attacked for the administration's policy regarding Korea. In
defining the American "defensive
perimeter" in the Far East in
January, 1950, Acheson excluded both Formosa and Korea
from the areas that the United
States agreed to defend. That
June, the North Korean Communists attacked South Korea,
touching off the Korean War.
After his resignation from the
State Department in 1953, he
returned to his law practice and,
as an elder statesman of the
Democratic Party, also served
as a spokesman and consultant
on foreign policy to Presidents
John F. Kennedy and **Lyndon B.
Johnson** (*see both*). His writings
include *Pattern of Responsibility*
(1952), *A Democrat Looks at His
Party* (1955), *A Citizen Looks at
Congress* (1957), *Power and
Diplomacy* (1958), *Sketches
from Life of Men I Have Known*
(1961), and *Present at the Creation: My Years in the State Department* (1969), which won the
Pulitzer Prize for History in
1970.

AGNEW, Spiro Theodore (born
1918). Relatively unknown outside his native state of Maryland
before he was chosen as the
running mate of **Richard M.
Nixon** (*see*) in 1968, Agnew has
emerged as the leading defender
of the Nixon administration
against attacks by critics. The
Vice-President was born in
Maryland, the son of an immigrant Greek restaurateur whose
name was originally Anagnostopoulos. He studied chemistry
for three years (1937–1940) at
Johns Hopkins University before transferring to the University of Baltimore Law School.
While attending night classes,
he worked by day as an insurance-company clerk, supermar-

ket manager, and claims adjustor. Agnew's education was interrupted by World War II. He became an infantry company commander in France and Germany and won a Bronze Star Medal. After the war, Agnew completed his law studies, earning his degree in 1947. He opened a law office and, although formerly a registered Democrat, became active in the Republican Party. In 1957, he was appointed to the Baltimore County Zoning Board of Appeals. After the Democratic Party gained control of the county four years later, he ran for the post of county executive. Campaigning on a reform platform, he was the first Republican to win that office in 67 years. After compiling an impressive record in building new schools and other county improvements, Agnew sought the governorship of Maryland in 1966. He decisively defeated his Democratic opponent, an avowed segregationist, and in his first year as governor won legislative approval of most of his campaign promises. Among his achievements were a tax-reform law that was designed to create revenues for antipoverty programs, an open-housing law, and the elimination of a state ban on interracial marriages. In addition, a liberalized abortion law and what was at that time the nation's stiffest water-pollution controls were enacted. Agnew's reputation as a liberal was reversed in his second year as governor. He had 227 Negro students arrested when they staged a sit-in in the statehouse at Annapolis in April, 1968, and then chastised a group of 80 Negro leaders—many of them his supporters—for not speaking out against militant blacks. In cutting the state budget, he heavily trimmed health and welfare funds, and he demanded and received the power to call out the state militia when

rioting seemed imminent. Although an early supporter of Governor Nelson A. Rockefeller (born 1908) of New York, Agnew switched to Nixon's camp after Rockefeller declined to campaign actively for the Republican Presidential nomination in 1968. Agnew subsequently placed Nixon's name in nomination when the party convention was held that August. The next day, after discarding several other prospects, Nixon asked Agnew to run for the Vice-Presidency. During and since that victorious election campaign against Democrats **Hubert H. Humphrey** and **Edmund S. Muskie** (*see both*), Agnew has taken the "hard line." In October, 1969, in an appeal to the "silent majority" of Americans who reportedly backed Nixon's policy in Vietnam, Agnew attacked critics of the war as "an effete corps of impudent snobs." A month later, he was highly critical of the way the nation's major broadcasting networks and leading newspapers reported the war and other administration policies. Although he had been a butt of jokes after his nomination ("Spiro Who?" was a common question), Agnew has since become well known throughout the nation for his frank expression of his opinions. "It is time" he has declared, "for Americans to return to the hard, fresh realism and to the unique mix of optimism and pragmatism that made America a great power."

B

BAY OF PIGS INVASION. The first major international crisis faced by President **John F. Kennedy** (*see*) occurred on April 17, 1961—only three months after he took office—when approximately 1,000 Cuban exiles, supported by American aircraft,

invaded their homeland at the *Bahia de Cochinos* (Bay of Pigs) in an attempt to overthrow the government of Premier Fidel Castro (born 1927). The Cuban refugees had been preparing for the invasion under the guidance of the U.S. Central Intelligence Agency (C.I.A.) during the administration of President **Dwight D. Eisenhower** (*see*). As early as October, 1960, news reports from Guatemala, where the C.I.A. was training the invasion forces, reached the United States but created little stir. The New York *Times* received an account of the invasion plans from a correspondent but did not print it because its editors believed it would jeopardize national security. Kennedy, who had had grave misgivings about the mission, later declared that he was sorry that the *Times* had not disclosed its information. The C.I.A. and military experts had assured him that a large number of Cubans were eager to unseat Castro, and that the project would succeed without deeply involving the United States. Kennedy finally agreed to the operation. However, Castro's strength had been underestimated, and within three days of the landing most of the invaders had been captured. As a result, the United States, which had shown itself to be powerless in the face of a small and supposedly weak adversary, lost prestige throughout the world. The C.I.A. fell under censure for meddling in the internal affairs of another country, and for initiating, rather than carrying out, foreign policy. The impact of the Bay of Pigs invasion was felt as late as 1968, when Cuban exiles in the United States who had become American citizens voted heavily for **Richard M. Nixon** (*see*) because, it is thought, they still blamed the Democrats for not intervening with troops to topple Castro.

BERLIN AIRLIFT. From June, 1948, until May, 1949, the Allies were forced to airlift supplies to Berlin in order to prevent the starvation of 2,500,000 Berliners or a Russian take-over of the city. In the last week of June, 1948, the Soviet Union halted all land and water transportation between Berlin and the western zones of occupied Germany. Like all Germany, Berlin had been divided into zones of occupation following the Nazi defeat in World War II, but the city as a whole lay within the Russian-controlled sector and was about 100 miles from the nearest Allied border. Soviet Premier Joseph Stalin (1879–1953) ordered the blockade of Berlin in the hope of bringing the city under complete Russian control. Faced with the alternative of abandoning Berlin or fighting to preserve its status, General Lucius D. Clay (born 1897), the U.S. military governor, sent for General Curtis LeMay (born 1906), commander of the air forces in Europe, to determine the possibility of flying in supplies for the American garrison. Acting on LeMay's advice, President **Harry S. Truman** (*see*) gave the order for the airlift to proceed. Initially, C-47 cargo planes, capable of carrying three tons of foodstuffs and medical supplies each, were used to supply the garrison. It soon became apparent that the Allies would have to feed the entire city of 2,500,000 people. By mid-July, 1,500 tons a day were being flown in by the Americans and 500 tons a day by the British. The planes took off from Frankfurt and Wiesbaden to land at Tempelhof airfield in the American sector, Gatow airfield in the British sector, and, after November, Tegel airfield in the French sector. As the weather grew colder and more supplies of coal became necessary also, the tonnage requirements increased to

7,000 tons a day. By December, 300 C-54s, capable of carrying 10 tons each, were available for use. Night and day, despite bad weather, the weariness of pilots, and accidents (61 airmen were killed during the 11 months), the deliveries continued. On Easter Sunday, 1949, a record total of 1,398 flights were made (one plane landing every 62 seconds), and 12,941 tons were delivered. A month later, on May 12, 1949, the crisis ended when the Russian government finally abandoned its blockade of Berlin. The airlift, however, was continued for three more months in case the blockade was resumed. In all, 2,300,000 tons of food and coal supplies had been flown into the city on 276,-926 flights. However, the split between East and West Germany became more permanent. A democratic West German government, the Federal Republic of Germany, was established on September 21, 1949. A month later, the Russians established a puppet regime, the German Democratic Republic, in East Germany.

BETHUNE, Mary McLeod (1875–1955). A well-known Negro educator who founded Bethune-Cookman College in Daytona Beach, Florida, Mrs. Bethune was a special adviser on minority affairs to President Franklin D. Roosevelt (1882–1945) and directed the Division of Negro Affairs in the National Youth Administration from 1936 to 1944. In addition, she served as a consultant on interracial affairs at the first conference of the United Nations in San Francisco. Born in South Carolina, Mrs. Bethune graduated from Moody Bible Institute in Chicago and then began a career in education in 1897. She was married to Albert Bethune in 1899. Mrs. Bethune taught at schools in Georgia and Florida until 1903.

The following year, she established the all-Negro Daytona Normal and Industrial School for Girls, raising money for the venture by persuading wealthy businessmen to contribute funds—as well as by selling fried fish and sweet-potato pies door to door. The school later became Bethune-Cookman College, with Mrs. Bethune serving as president from its founding until 1942. A leader in many cultural, educa-

Mary McLeod Bethune

tional, and governmental organizations, Mrs. Bethune founded the National Council of Negro Women, was an important figure in the National Association for the Advancement of Colored People (N.A.A.C.P.), and served as vice-president of the Commission on Interracial Cooperation of the National Urban League. She was a close friend of Eleanor Roosevelt (1884–1962) and represented President **Harry S. Truman** (*see*) at a presidential inauguration in Liberia. During World War II, Mrs. Bethune assisted the Secretary of War in choosing the first Officers Candidate Schools for Wacs. She was the recipient of numerous awards and honorary degrees for her contributions to interracial harmony in the United States.

BROWN VS. BOARD OF EDUCATION of Topeka, Kansas. *See* **Civil-rights Movement; Warren, Earl.**

BUNCHE, Ralph Johnson (born 1904). The grandson of a slave, Bunche became a diplomat of world renown and a winner of the Nobel Peace Prize for efforts to restore peace in the Middle East. Born in Michigan, Bunche graduated from the University of California in 1927. Receiving a master's degree in government from Harvard the following year, he became an instructor of political science at Howard University in Washington, D.C. At the age of 25, he was named chairman of the department. Leaving Howard in 1932, Bunche returned to Harvard for a doctorate in government. A two-year postdoctoral fellowship (1936–1937) then enabled him to further his studies in anthropology and colonial policy at Northwestern University, the London School of Economics, and the University of Capetown in South Africa. Upon returning home in 1938, Bunche became a researcher at the Carnegie Corporation, where he helped prepare *The American Dilemma* (1944), a noted study of the American Negro. He resumed teaching at Howard in 1940. After America's entry into World War II in 1941, Bunche joined the staff of the Office of Strategic Services (O.S.S.) as a senior social-science analyst. One year later, he became chief research analyst in the African and Far Eastern section of the O.S.S. In 1944, Bunche entered the State Department as an Area Specialist. An expert on Africa and dependent areas, he helped draft the sections on non-self-governing territories and trustee-

ships that were later written into the charter of the United Nations. In 1945, Bunche was appointed associate chief of the Division of Dependent Area Affairs. From July to October of that year, he was acting chief, the first Negro to become an acting division chief in the history of the State Department. In March, 1947, Bunche became director of the Trusteeship Division of the U.N. Secretariat. At the time of his appointment, the New York *Herald Tribune* commented that "he is as well qualified as is humanly possible for the post." In December of that year, Bunche was named chief secretary to the U.N. Palestine Commission. Following the assassination of Count Folke Bernadotte (1895–1948), the U.N. mediator in the Palestine dispute, Bunche was made acting mediator. His successful negotiation of the Israeli-Egyptian armistice in 1949 earned him the Nobel Peace Prize in 1950. Bunche was the first Negro to be so honored. In 1955, Bunche was appointed an Undersecretary of the U.N. and two years later was named U.N. Undersecretary for special political affairs, the highest position ever held by an American in the Secretariat. He supervised the U.N. emergency force organized to mediate the Suez crisis in 1956 and four years later played an active role in settling the Congo crisis. He retired in 1971 because of ill health. In addition to his duties at the U.N., Bunche wrote frequent articles on politics.

C

CIVIL RIGHTS ACT OF 1964. *See* **Civil-rights Movement.**

CIVIL-RIGHTS MOVEMENT. The civil-rights movement emerged as a national issue on May 17, 1954, when the Su-

preme Court unanimously ruled in *Brown vs. Board of Education of Topeka, Kansas* that segregation in public schools was unconstitutional. The ruling, based on the Fourteenth Amendment's guarantee of "equal protection of the laws," overturned the 1896 Court decision that permitted "separate but equal" facilities for Negroes. With the landmark 1954 ruling, efforts were renewed to secure for blacks the freedoms promised after the Civil War that had been stymied for nearly 90 years in both the North and the South. In the South, Negroes were deprived of the right to vote, to use the same facilities as whites, to eat in the same restaurants, and to work in many factories, as well as to attend the same schools. In the North, blacks were often discriminated against in jobs and were crowded into slums because of unwritten restrictions barring them from white neighborhoods. So-called de facto segregation resulted in all-black schools because those that Negroes attended were situated in exclusively Negro areas. The Court's ruling awakened the nation's more than 15,000,000 blacks to demand "Freedom Now." At the time, 2,500,000 Negroes were attending all-black schools in 17 Southern states and the District of Columbia. Thirteen years later, in 1967, as the nation's population swelled, there were still 2,600,000 Negroes attending segregated schools, and only 16% of Negro students in 11 of those Southern states were in integrated classes. What integration had taken place had often occurred against the backdrop of armed troops. President **Dwight D. Eisenhower** (*see*) was forced to send federal forces to Little Rock, Arkansas, in 1957 to desegregate that city's Central High School in the face of resistance by Governor Orval E.

Faubus (born 1910). Federal troops had to be used to enroll the first Negro, James H. Meredith (born 1933), at the University of Mississippi in 1962, and the following year federal marshals were needed when Governor **George C. Wallace** (*see*) personally blocked the registration of two Negroes at the University of Alabama. The struggle for equality grew in intensity and in violence as progress seemed to move so slowly and despite a number of important laws enacted by Congress, including two voting-rights measures in 1957 and 1960 during Eisenhower's administration. Each civil-rights measure enacted by Congress came as a reaction to growing Negro demands for immediate action. In the meantime, the black community split into warring factions. Since its inception in 1910, the National Association for the Advancement of Colored People (N.A.A.C.P.) fought to achieve racial equality by legal means—through legislation and court orders. Its counsel, **Thurgood Marshall** (*see*), later the first Negro to serve on the Supreme Court, was instrumental in winning the 1954 Court ruling on public schools. Similarly, the Reverend Dr. **Martin Luther King, Jr.** (*see*), a Nobel Peace Prize-winning advocate of nonviolence, sought to bring about change by passive resistance to discriminatory local laws in the form of boycotts, sit-ins, marches, and picketing. Freedom rides throughout the South, first sponsored by the Congress of Racial Equality (CORE) in 1961, were designed to desegregate public buses and depots. "We shall overcome" became the rallying song of these demonstrations, the most famous of which was the March on Washington on August 28, 1963, when more than 200,000 whites and blacks gathered at the Lincoln Memorial to hear Dr. King and other rights leaders urge prompt action. President **Lyndon B. Johnson** (*see*) used the same words—"We shall overcome"—in his plea for rights legislation. Although a Southerner whose past record on civil rights was undistinguished, Johnson, as President, was forceful in seeking laws to eliminate social injustices—the Civil Rights Act of 1964 and the Voting Rights Act of 1965. In 1966, the last

Poster, made by children in Wisconsin, manifests the new racial pride.

poll tax, the $2 fee required to vote in Mississippi, was dropped, and three years later Charles

Evers (born 1920), the brother of slain rights leader Medgar Evers (1925–1963), became the first Negro mayor of Fayette, Mississippi. However, young militant blacks became disillusioned by the slow pace of integration and the continued suppression of their efforts by brutality, such as had occurred in April, 1963, when police in Birmingham, Alabama, used dogs and fire hoses to break up a peaceful march. The militants finally broke with the N.A.A.C.P. and Dr. King in 1966 to form "black power" movements, the most radical of which became the Black Panthers. Their hostility was intensified by the slayings of four major rights figures within five years after the March on Washington—the assassinations of President **John F. Kennedy** (*see*) in November, 1963, of black nationalist leader **Malcolm X** (*see*) in 1965, and of both Dr. King and **Robert F. Kennedy** (*see*) in 1968. In addition, bombings, intimidation, and the murder of rights workers—such as the three college students engaged in a voter registration drive in Mississippi in 1964—increased tensions. Racial unrest was not confined to the South. There were riots not only in such cities as Birmingham and Selma, Alabama, Cambridge, Maryland, Atlanta, Georgia, and Bogalusa, Louisiana, but in the North as well. The most serious of the "long, hot summer" outbreaks occurred in the Harlem ghetto of New York in 1964, in the Watts section of Los Angeles in 1965, in Detroit and Newark in 1967, and in Cleveland in 1968. That same year, a special Presidential commission on civil disorders reported that the nation "is moving toward two societies, one black, one white—separate but unequal." By then, the campaign for equal rights in housing, schools, and jobs was, many

Negroes believed, being side-tracked by America's growing involvement in the Vietnam war. Antipoverty programs designed to create equal job and school opportunities had to contest for government funds with the mounting war effort. As a result, black leaders as diverse as Dr. King and Stokeley Carmichael (born 1941), a militant who was formerly with the Student Non-violent Coordinating Committee, began backing antiwar protests. At the same time, many blacks—including H. Rap Brown (born 1943), Eldridge Cleaver (born 1935), and Bobby Seale (born 1936)—sought to rid themselves of white standards and attitudes by identifying themselves with Afro-American movements. James Forman (born 1929) demanded, and sometimes received, "reparations" from white churches for past injustices done to Negroes. Black extremism eventually touched off a "backlash" among many white Americans, and "law and order" became a central issue of the 1968 Presidential campaign. The effectiveness of the backlash vote was evidenced in the third-party candidacy of segregationist George Wallace and in the victory of **Richard M. Nixon** (*see*), which was based on a coalition of conservative Republican and Southern support. Although Nixon was blocked in his attempt to appoint two Southerners—Clement F. Haynsworth, Jr. (born 1912), and G. Harrold Carswell (born 1919)—to the Supreme Court, his administration did slow efforts to force integration in the South. In October, 1969, the Court ruled that all public schools must be desegregated immediately. It later approved the busing of pupils as a way to achieve integration, but Nixon, in the summer of 1971, curtailed plans to enforce the ruling.

D

DEWEY, Thomas Edmund (1902–1971). This well-known "racket buster" and former Republican governor of New York was generally predicted to be the victor in the Presidential election of 1948. However, in a spectacular political upset, Dewey was defeated by his Democratic opponent, **Harry S. Truman** (*see*). A native of Owosso, Michigan, Dewey graduated from the University of Michigan in 1923 and received a law degree from Columbia University two years later. He subsequently practiced law in New York City until 1931, when he was appointed chief assistant to the U.S. attorney for the Southern District of New York. After briefly serving as a U.S. attorney (1933), Dewey in 1935 became a special prosecutor, assigned to conduct a two-year investigation of organized crime in New York. Although underworld lords initially derided him as a "boy scout," Dewey soon earned a nationwide reputation for his successful drives against narcotics, the vice traffic, and the notorious group of for-hire gunmen, Murder Incorporated. He obtained convictions in all but one of 73 cases. Dewy continued his racket-busting activities as district attorney of New York County from 1937 to 1941, and in 1942 he was elected to the first of three successive terms (1943–1955) as governor. Dewey achieved a record of efficiency, economy, and political moderation in state administration. As a result, he received the Republican Presidential nomination in 1944. He lost the election to Franklin D. Roosevelt (1882–1945) by 432 electoral votes to 99 but polled more than 22,000,-000 popular votes—the largest number cast for a Republican in

Thomas E. Dewey

16 years. Dewey again became his party's candidate in 1948 and campaigned energetically throughout the nation, coining the slogan "It's time for a change." Political analysts were so certain that he would beat Truman that the Chicago *Daily Tribune* ran its front-page election story with the headline "DEWEY DEFEATS TRUMAN" even before all the polls closed. However, Dewey's delay in taking a forceful stance on a number of issues, and the defection of supposedly secure Republican states in the Middle West, contributed to another Democratic victory, with Truman gaining a margin of more than 2,000,000 popular votes and winning 303

electoral votes to Dewey's 189. Dewey subsequently disclaimed any further Presidential aspirations and reentered state politics. As leader of the Eastern wing of the Republican Party, Dewey helped engineer the nomination of General **Dwight D. Eisenhower** (*see*) at the Republican National Convention in 1952. At the end of his third term as governor in 1955, Dewey retired from public life and returned to his law practice. He remained an elder statesman of his party.

DIRKSEN, Everett McKinley (1896–1969). One of the few great orators to serve in Congress in modern times—always quick to spice his remarks with biblical allusions—Dirksen was a Representative for 16 years before being elected in 1950 to the Senate, where he served until his death. He was the most influential Republican in Congress after he became his party's Senate leader in 1959, and was noted for his many policy reversals in matters pertaining to both foreign and domestic affairs. The jowly, shock-haired Dirksen became a leading spokesman for Republican policy during the Democratic administrations of **John F. Kennedy** and **Lyndon B. Johnson** (*see both*). Born in Pekin, Illinois, Dirksen served with the army in France during World War I and subsequently held several minor offices in Illinois before entering Congress in 1933. In Washington, Dirksen attended night school and received his law degree in 1936. The ability to make rapid aboutfaces for ideological reasons or when he deemed it expedient was second nature to him. For example, he voted against many New Deal measures advocated by President Franklin D. Roosevelt (1882–1945) but supported the Social Security Act (1935) and the Minimum Wage Act

(1938). In foreign policy, Dirksen at first was an isolationist. However, a few months before the Japanese attacked Pearl Harbor on December 7, 1941, he reversed his stand and urged all Republicans to show "a unity of purpose" by backing Roosevelt's foreign policy. In 1954, Dirksen supported Senator **Joseph R. McCarthy** (*see*) of Wisconsin in the face of mounting nationwide opposition to McCarthy's campaign against alleged Communist infiltration of the State Department. Dirksen subsequently became famous for three major policy reversals. In 1962, he

UPI

Everett M. Dirksen

abandoned his critical stand concerning the administration's request for authority to buy United Nations bonds in order to make up deficits that were largely the result of French and Soviet refusals to make peacekeeping payments to the U.N. "I will not charge my conscience with any act or deed which would contribute to the foundering of the United Nations," he declared. The following year, Dirksen initially opposed the

ratification of the nuclear testban treaty, but after additional study and consideration he voted for it. In March, 1964, Dirksen, who always had enormous respect for property rights, attacked the Civil Rights Act, mainly because he opposed the granting to the federal government of powers to enforce nondiscrimination in public housing and jobs. However, two months later, in another historic reversal, he supported the bill, commandeering enough Republican votes—27 out of 33—to secure its passage. Dirksen's own efforts to secure adoption of a constitutional amendment permitting prayers in public schools proved fruitless.

DOUGLAS, William Orville (born 1898). Considered the most liberal member of the Supreme Court during the last 30 years, Douglas has frequently dissented from the other Justices in defending the civil liberties guaranteed by the First Amendment to the Constitution. Douglas was born in Minnesota and grew up in the state of Washington, where he became a lifelong enthusiast for hiking and camping. After graduating from Columbia Law School in 1925, he worked for a Wall Street law firm and, in 1928, joined the faculty of Yale Law School. There he became a specialist in business law, which led to his appointment to the Securities and Exchange Commission in 1934 by Joseph P. Kennedy (1888–1969), then chairman of the S.E.C. On the S.E.C., Douglas, who was an advocate of the New Deal, pursued a policy of reform, investigating bankrupt businesses and reorganizing the nation's stock exchanges. He served as the commission's chairman from 1936 to 1939. That year, President Franklin D. Roosevelt (1882–1945) named Douglas, then 40, to the Supreme Court. The youngest Justice to be named to the Court in 125 years, Douglas soon earned a reputation for his liberal views, his brilliance, and his colorful character. A close friend of the President's, Douglas was one of the two men whom Roosevelt considered for a running mate in the elections of 1944. **Harry S. Truman** (*see*) was finally chosen and, when Roosevelt died the next year, became President. Many years later, Douglas, in retrospect, said in an interview that had he been Roosevelt's Vice-President, "there would have been no Hiroshima" and the cold war with the Soviet Union might have been avoided. On the bench, Douglas' legal opinions have expressed his belief that "The American government is premised on the theory that if the mind of man is to be free, his ideas, his beliefs, his ideology, his philosophy must be placed beyond the reach of government." Associate Justice Hugo Black (1886–1971) shared Douglas' views and, during the so-called McCarthy era in the early 1950s, when the fear of Communist influence in government was widespread, the two Justices constantly disagreed with the majority of the Court, which upheld government restrictions on free speech. Douglas maintained that even Communists had the right to free speech. In 1953, Douglas tried to stay the execution of two spies who had sold nuclear secrets to Russia, Julius Rosenberg and his wife, Ethel (*see* **Rosenberg spy case**). As a result, an unsuccessful attempt was made by conservatives in the House of Representatives to impeach him. A second effort was made to impeach Douglas because of his "moral character" after he married his fourth wife in 1966. Douglas never cared whether his decisions were popular and, as late as 1968, he was the only Justice to oppose upholding a federal statute prohibiting the burning of draft cards as a protest against the Vietnam war. When Associate Justice **Abe Fortas** (*see*) resigned from the Supreme Court in May, 1969, over his questionable judicial conduct in accepting money from a private source, Douglas likewise fell under fire for receiving outside income from the Albert Parvin Foundation. The foundation, which sponsors educational programs and international meetings of jurors, scholars, and politicians, derives some of its funds from Las Vegas gambling casinos. Although Douglas asserted that the charges against him were "manufactured" to force him off the Supreme Court because of his liberal politics, he subsequently resigned as the foundation's president and director. In July, 1969, the American Bar Association announced, following an investigation, that there was insufficient evidence to judge his involvement with the foundation. In 1970, an effort was undertaken to impeach him for his sympathetic statements about young revolutionaries, but it failed in the House.

DULLES, John Foster (1888–1959). As Secretary of State from 1953 to 1959 under President **Dwight D. Eisenhower** (*see*), Dulles dominated the formulation and carrying out of American foreign policy to a greater extent than any previous holder of that office. A militant anti-Communist, he considered neutralism immoral, advocated the "liberation" of Communist-held areas of Eastern Europe, and believed that the threat of massive nuclear retaliation would be enough to prevent Communist aggression. These policies, coupled with his determination to go "to the brink" of nuclear war, if necessary, made him an extremely controversial world figure. Dulles was accused of "brinkmanship" after promising the peoples of Soviet-dominated Eastern Europe in January, 1953, that they could "count on us." However, the following June, when East German workers rioted, and in 1956 during the Hungarian uprising against Russia, he took no steps to help "liberate" either people. Born into a wealthy and socially prominent family in Washington, D.C., Dulles spent much of his youth in the capital with his grandfather, John Watson Foster (1836–1917), who was Secretary of State in 1892 under President Benjamin Harrison (1833–1901). This afforded him early contact with Washington society as well as the workings of American foreign policy. In the summer of 1907, Dulles accompanied his grandfather to the second Hague Peace Conference in the Netherlands, where he developed the strong interest in diplomacy that he held for the rest of his life. Dulles graduated from Princeton University in 1908 and subsequently studied law at George Washington University Law School before he was admitted to the New York bar in 1911. During World War I, he served as a captain on the War Industries Board, and in 1919 was legal counsel to the American delegation to the reparations committee at the Paris Peace Conference. Dulles then returned to the practice of law, serving as a financial consultant to several foreign governments. In the late 1930s, he began a long political association with the Republican politician, **Thomas E. Dewey** (*see*), and helped plan Dewey's strategy in his unsuccessful bid for his party's Presidential nomination in 1940. Four years later, when

Dewey won the nomination, he became his adviser on foreign policy. The following year, Dulles became senior United States adviser at the San Francisco conference that drafted the charter of the United Nations. He occasionally served as a delegate to the U.N. General Assembly from 1946 to 1950. In July, 1949, Dewey, then governor of New York, appointed Dulles to complete the Senate term of Robert F. Wagner, Sr. (1877–1953), who had resigned, but Dulles lost the seat in a special election held the following November. In 1950, President **Harry S. Truman** (*see*) named him ambassador-at-large, and as such he was the chief author and negotiator of the Japanese Peace Treaty of 1951. Dulles formulated the Republican foreign-policy platform for the election of 1952 and was one of the first men Eisenhower appointed to his cabinet after his election. During his six years as Secretary of State, Dulles enjoyed an unprecedented degree of authority because of the President's confidence in him and America's prestige as the major world power. He traveled more than any other Secretary of State, flying more than 500,000 miles on missions throughout the world. Dulles created a network of local treaties—his critics accused him of "pactomania"—designed to align the United States with as many non-Communist nations as possible, even those with Fascist governments. The two most important international organizations that Dulles helped forge were the Central Treaty Organization (CENTO) in the Middle East and the **Southeast Asia Treaty Organization** (*see*), both established in 1954. In the Far East, Dulles and Eisenhower refused to help the French in Vietnam in 1954. They also declined in 1954–55 to

provide military support to help Nationalist China defend the offshore islands of Quemoy and Matsu against the Communist Chinese on the ground that intervention might lead to an atomic war. However, Dulles pledged the United States to protect Taiwan. In the Middle East, Dulles provided Egypt with economic aid but would not sell it arms. In July, 1956, when he realized that Egypt was drifting more and more into the Soviet sphere of influence, he withdrew America's offer for financial support of the huge Aswan Dam project on the Nile River, the key to Egypt's vital irrigation program. The Egyptian government countered the following week by nationalizing the Suez Canal. As a result, in late October Britain and France joined Israel in invading Egypt. American opposition to the attack helped force the invaders to withdraw and temporarily improved the United States' relations with Egypt. However, Dulles soon adopted a more supportive stand toward Britain, France, Israel, and other allies in the Middle East. This new policy was incorporated in the so-called Eisenhower Doctrine of January, 1957, which was largely the handiwork of Dulles. The President announced that the United States would give economic aid and was "prepared to use armed force" in the Middle East in the event of "aggression from any country controlled by international Communism." This doctrine was invoked in May, 1958, when the United States sent marines into Lebanon after pro-Egyptian elements threatened its government. Due to ill health, Dulles had to resign his position in April, 1959. He died of abdominal cancer the following month. Dulles published *War, Peace, and Change* (1939) and *War or Peace* (1950).

E

EISENHOWER, Dwight David (*Continued from Volume 15*). A national hero following his achievements as Supreme Commander of Allied forces in Western Europe during World War II, Eisenhower was courted by the Democrats, who wanted him to run as their Presidential candidate in 1948. The General refused and, instead, accepted the presidency of Columbia University. Over the next four years, he took several leaves of absence from Columbia to serve as a military adviser in Washington, D.C., and as Supreme Commander of the armed forces of the **North Atlantic Treaty Organization** (*see*) from 1950 to 1952.

A 1952 Eisenhower campaign button

Eisenhower was finally persuaded by Republican politicians to become their party's candidate for President in 1952. After resigning from NATO, he waged a close campaign against Senator Robert A. Taft (1889–1953) and won the Republican nomination in July, 1952. In what was essentially a personality contest with his Democratic opponent, **Adlai E. Stevenson** (*see*), Eisenhower pledged to "clean up the mess in Washington," balance the budget, and end the Korean War. That November, he polled about 34,000,000 popular votes, almost

7,000,000 more than Stevenson, and won 442 electoral votes to Stevenson's 89. Eisenhower's election as the 34th President of the United States returned the Republicans to power for the first time in 20 years. Eisenhower believed in private enterprise and more local control of government affairs and espoused a policy of "moderate Republicanism" in domestic affairs. During his administrations, he was able to get enacted legislative programs for the establishment of a Department of Health, Education, and Welfare, a federal highway system, expanded Social Security benefits, increased minimum wages, urban renewal, and the development of water resources. Price and wage controls imposed during the Korean War were eliminated, foreign aid was scaled down, and, in order to balance the budget and cut taxes, the federal payroll was reduced. Using the same methods he employed as the head of Allied forces in Europe, Eisenhower delegated much of his responsibilities to his Secretary of State, **John Foster Dulles,** his Vice-President, **Richard M. Nixon** (*see both*), and other cabinet and White House advisers. Having vowed to personally visit Korea, Eisenhower traveled there in December, 1952, and, with Dulles, negotiated a truce in the Korean War in July, 1953. An internationalist, Eisenhower also committed himself to the security of West Germany and tried to improve relationships with the Middle East, the Far East, and Latin America. He presented an "Atoms for Peace" proposal to the United Nations in 1953, and in 1954 helped found the **Southeast Asia Treaty Organization** (*see*), a defensive alliance against Communist aggression in the Pacific. In 1955, he attended the Geneva Summit Conference with British Prime Minister Anthony Eden (born 1897), French Premier Edgar Faure (born 1908), and Russian leaders Nikita Khrushchev (1894–1971) and Nikolai Bulganin (born 1895). The reunification of Germany, European security, disarmament, and cultural and trade exchanges were discussed. Although no agreements were reached, the meeting closed on a note of optimism, and Eisenhower's statements gave the world renewed hope for peace. In January, 1957, the President announced the "Eisenhower Doctrine," pledging America's use of force if necessary to protect the Middle East from Communist aggression. During 1953 and 1954, Eisenhower was faced with a growing controversy over Senator **Joseph R. McCarthy** (*see*) of Wisconsin, who was conducting an investigation into communism in the government. The President chided McCarthy for his "witch-hunt" tactics but did nothing to curb his activities. Then Eisenhower suffered a heart attack in September, 1955. It was the first of several major illnesses that he was to have while in office. He nevertheless decided to run for a second term in 1956. Campaigning on his record of peace and prosperity—which was enhanced by his insistence on a cease-fire and the withdrawal of French and British troops from the Suez Canal in October, 1956—Eisenhower again defeated Stevenson. This time he received 35,600,000 votes to Stevenson's 26,000,000 and 384 more electoral votes than Stevenson. From 1955 through the end of his second administration in 1961, Eisenhower had to contend with a Democrat-controlled Congress and with momentous problems at home and abroad. In September, 1957, he was forced to dispatch federal troops to Little Rock, Arkansas, to enforce a federal court order desegregating a local high school, an action that was applauded in the North but that antagonized Southerners. In October, 1957, the Soviet Union orbited its first unmanned satellite, Sputnik I, thus causing doubts throughout the world about American technical superiority. Business slumped sharply in the winter of 1957–58 and only slowly recovered. In the summer of 1958, Sherman Adams (born 1899), a Presidential assistant and one of Eisenhower's closest friends, was accused of peddling influence in federal agencies on behalf of his friends and was forced to resign. With Eisenhower's prestige at a low during the Congressional elections of November, 1958, the Democrats won control of Congress by the widest margin since 1936 and subsequently thwarted some of the President's programs. Eisenhower's talks with Khrushchev, who was then premier, in September, 1959, during the latter's visit to the United States, produced a temporary thaw in the cold war. However, the following May's "U-2 incident," in which an American high-altitude reconnaisance plane was shot down over Russia, ended the détente and caused the collapse of a scheduled summit conference later that month. Although Eisenhower had hoped to improve ties with Latin-American nations, he was forced to break off diplomatic relations with Cuba in January, 1961, after Fidel Castro (born 1927) had confiscated U.S. landholdings and business concerns and had demanded a drastic cut in the personnel of the American Embassy in Havana. Eisenhower supported Vice-President Nixon in his unsuccessful campaign for the Presidency in 1960. After **John F. Kennedy** (*see*) entered office in January, 1961, Eisenhowever retired to his farm in Gettysburg, Pennsylvania, where, as elder statesman of both his party and the nation, he was often consulted. He died of heart failure on March 28, 1969, a month after undergoing abdominal surgery. He was buried in Abilene, Kansas, where the Eisenhower Presidential Library had been dedicated seven years earlier.

F

FORTAS, Abe (born 1910). A well-known liberal legal scholar and confidant of President **Lyndon B. Johnson** (*see*), Fortas became the first Justice in the nation's history to resign from the Supreme Court under the pressure of public criticism over an alleged breach of judicial ethics. Fortas was born in Memphis, Tennessee. He attended Southwestern College in Memphis, paying his tuition by playing the violin in a dance band. He graduated first in his class from Yale Law School in 1933 and afterward taught there. During the next four years, Fortas commuted to Washington, D.C., where he served on the Agricultural Adjustment Administration and the Securities Exchange Commission. He moved there in 1937 as a full-time consultant to the S.E.C. and the following year became director of its public-utilities division. At the age of 32 in 1942, he became Undersecretary of the Department of the Interior, and four years later he served as an adviser to the organizational meeting of the United Nations in San Francisco. In 1946, he left government service to join a legal firm later known as Arnold, Fortas & Porter. Fortas became wealthy representing large corporations and gained fame by winning cases that extended the consti-

Abe Fortas

tutional and legal protections of the poor, the criminally insane, government employees accused of being security risks, and teachers required to take loyalty oaths. Although he and Lyndon Johnson had met in the 1930s, the two became close friends only after 1948, when Fortas helped the Texan to win his first Senate election campaign by getting Johnson's name reinstated on the ballot after it had been dropped because of alleged voting irregularities. After Johnson became President in 1963, Fortas became one of his most trusted advisers. He helped the President to select his staff and also arranged placing Johnson's financial holdings into a trust. He tried to rescue the President from embarrassing situations in scandals involving two former White House aides—Bobby Baker (born 1927), who was accused of illegal business activ-

ities, and Walter Jenkins (born 1918), who was involved in a morals case. Fortas helped run Johnson's successful Presidential campaign in 1964, and in July of the following year, when Associate Justice **Arthur J. Goldberg** (*see*) resigned from his Supreme Court seat to become the U.S. delegate to the United Nations, Johnson offered Fortas the job. At the time, Fortas and his lawyer-wife, the former Carolyn Eugenia Aggers (born 1910), were earning a combined income of more than $200,000 a year. Fortas initially turned down the relatively low-paying $39,500-a-year post. However, at Johnson's urging, he changed his mind and was sworn in that October, thus continuing the tradition started by Louis Brandeis (1856–1941) half a century earlier of having at least one Justice of Jewish faith on the Court. Fortas continued to see the President and advise him on appointees and legislative matters. In addition, soon after he joined the Supreme Court, he agreed to receive a $20,000-a-year lifetime fee as a consultant to the family foundation of Florida financier Louis E. Wolfson (born 1912). Fortas advised Wolfson on different occasions and received his first $20,000 check in January, 1966. That June, finding his judicial duties too time-consuming and learning that the government was about to indict Wolfson, Fortas resigned from the foundation and returned the check in December. The first hint that Fortas might have violated the separation of powers guaranteed in the Constitution in his close relationship with the President came in September, 1968, when the Senate refused to confirm Johnson's nomination of Fortas to succeed **Earl Warren** (*see*) as Chief Justice. In May, 1969, Fortas' connection with Wolfson. who was then serving a one-year jail sentence for selling unregistered securities, was disclosed by *Life* magazine. During the nationwide controversy that followed, there was talk of further revelations, investigations, and impeachment. On May 15, Fortas, who maintained that "There has been no wrong doing on my part," resigned from the Supreme Court. He returned to his law practice.

FROST, Robert Lee (1874–1963). One of the nation's greatest poets and the recipient of four Pulitzer Prizes, Frost wrote about the character, people, and life of New England, finding

UPI

Robert Frost

universal significance in all his subjects. Born in San Francisco, Frost moved to New England when he was 10 years old and lived there most of his life. He studied briefly at Dartmouth College and at Harvard University and worked as a bobbin boy in a Massachusetts cotton mill. He also worked as a shoemaker, a newspaper editor, a schoolteacher, and a farmer. His main ambition, however, was to be a poet, and he went to England in 1912 because he be-

lieved the British were more appreciative of poets. During his three years there, he published his first two volumes—both about New England—*A Boy's Will* (1913) and *North of Boston* (1914). *North of Boston* contains many of his most famous poems, including "Mending Wall," "Home Burial," and "The Death of the Hired Man." Upon returning to America in 1915, Frost settled on a New Hampshire farm. The following year, he published *Mountain Interval,* a collection that included "Birches" and "The Road Not Taken." The latter contains the lines that indicated the direction of his own life:

> Two roads diverged in a wood,
>   and I—
> I took the one less traveled by,
>   And that has made all the dif-
>   ference.

In 1924, Frost was awarded the first of his four Pulitzer Prizes for *New Hampshire* (1923), a volume of poems that includes "Stopping by Woods on a Snowy Evening" and "Fire and Ice." His other prize-winning collections were *Collected Poems* (1930), honored in 1931; *A Further Range* (1936), the winner in 1937; and *A Witness Tree* (1942), honored in 1943. Frost also taught and lectured at several colleges and universities, including Amherst College and Michigan and Harvard universities. In tribute to his lifework, Frost was asked to read a poem at the inauguration of President **John F. Kennedy** *(see)* on January 20, 1961. He wrote one especially for the occasion but stumbled over the lines and instead then recited his "The Gift Outright." When the gentle, white-haired poet died two years later at the age of 89, Kennedy said, "Frost leaves a vacancy in the American spirit."

FULBRIGHT, James William

(born 1905). A Rhodes scholar who sponsored the extensive program for the exchange of American and foreign teachers and students known as the Fulbright Act, this Democratic Senator from Arkansas became in the 1960s the spokesman for the so-called doves who opposed the war in Vietnam. Born in Missouri, Fulbright grew up in Arkansas and graduated from the University of Arkansas in 1925. As a Rhodes scholar, Fulbright studied history and political science at Oxford University in England until 1931. He earned a law degree at George Washington University in 1934 and worked in Washington, D.C., in the antitrust division of the Department of Justice. In 1936, Fulbright joined the faculty of his alma mater in Arkansas, becoming president in 1939. Always a controversial figure, he was dismissed two years later after a dispute with Governor Homer M. Adkins (1890–1964) over a faculty appointment. Fulbright was elected to the House of Representatives in 1942 and to his first term in the Senate in 1944. An internationalist and an early supporter of the United Nations, Fulbright introduced in 1945 a bill providing that the United States use the proceeds from the foreign sale of its surplus World War II property to finance an International Educational Exchange (I.E.E.) program for teachers and students to foster world understanding. President **Harry S. Truman** *(see)* signed the Fulbright Act into law on August 1, 1946, committing the government to its first large, long-term, and worldwide educational program. As of July 1, 1969, more than 17,000 Americans and 38,000 foreigners from some 150 nations and territories had received exchange grants. Although a liberal in foreign matters, Fulbright has remained popular among his constituents because he has supported states' rights. However, he was the only Senator to vote in 1954 against a

J. William Fulbright

$214,000 appropriation for Senator **Joseph R. McCarthy** (*see*) of Wisconsin to use in his inquiry into alleged Communist infiltration of the State Department. On the Senate floor, Fulbright likened McCarthy to an animal. In return, McCarthy labeled Fulbright "Senator Halfbright." Shortly before assuming the chairmanship of the Senate Foreign Relations Committee in 1959, Fulbright set forth his concept of the Senate's role in formulating foreign policy. He declared that the President was responsible for day-to-day decisions, but that the Senate should deal with fundamental problems and provide a forum for debating these problems at crucial times. In 1966, Fulbright became an outspoken critic of the way in which President **Lyndon B. Johnson** (*see*) was conducting the Vietnam War. During a bombing pause in January of that year, he argued that the Senate should be consulted before the bombing was

resumed, that the administration's "peace offensive" be continued, and that the rebel Vietcong be a party in peace negotiations. As a result, Fulbright was accused by "hawks," or supporters of the war, of making diplomatic concessions to the enemy and undermining the American war effort. He has continued to lead opposition to the war under President **Richard M. Nixon** (*see*), pressing for the immediate withdrawal of American forces from Vietnam.

G

GOLDBERG, Arthur Joseph (born 1908). A distinguished labor-management mediator and at one time Secretary of Labor, Goldberg has also served as an Associate Justice of the Supreme Court and ambassador to the United Nations. Goldberg was born and raised on Chicago's West Side, the son of Russian-immigrant parents. Determined to have a legal career, he worked nights at a post office to support himself while a student at Northwestern University Law School. At graduation, he was first in his class but too young to take the Illinois bar examination. However, he received special dispensation to take the test and was admitted to the bar in 1929. Goldberg worked in several Chicago law firms until he established his own practice in 1933. After defending the Chicago Newspaper Guild, which was on strike against the Hearst Corporation, he began to specialize in labor law. He subsequently represented a number of other unions, including the United Steelworkers, the United Packinghouse Workers, and the Amalgamated Clothing Workers. During World War II, Goldberg served as a liaison between the Office of Strategic Services

and the intelligence apparatus of the underground labor movement in Europe. Discharged in 1944 with the rank of major, he returned to his Chicago law practice. At the same time, he also began to lecture at the John Marshall Law School in Atlanta, Georgia, and the Chicago School of Industrial Relations. In 1948, Philip Murray (1886–1952), president of the Congress of Industrial Organizations, named Goldberg general counsel to the C.I.O. and the United Steelworkers Union. As such, he won in 1949 a court decision that held pensions were a valid concern in collective bargaining. Goldberg was a key figure in arranging the merger of the C.I.O. and the American Federation of Labor in 1955. He then urged the formation of an ethical practices committee to look into charges of corrupt union practices and served as a principal author of the A.F.L.-C.I.O. Code of Ethical Standards. He also spearheaded the fight to rid the labor federation of the corrupt International Brotherhood of Teamsters. During the 1960 Presidential campaign of **John F. Kennedy** (*see*), Goldberg helped to mobilize

Arthur J. Goldberg

organized labor to support the Democratic Party. Following his election, Kennedy appointed Goldberg Secretary of Labor, saying, "I cannot think of any American who brings greater competence in this field, longer experience, broader knowledge, and a greater devotion to public interest." As Secretary, Goldberg actively participated in the settlement of several major labor disputes, including a New York City harbor strike in 1961. The following year Kennedy named him an Associate Justice of the Supreme Court. Goldberg remained on the bench until 1965, when President **Lyndon B. Johnson** (*see*) appointed him the U.S. ambassador to the United Nations. Goldberg resigned his U.N. post three years later, stating that he could work for peace more effectively if he were "freed from the intense preoccupation" of his official position. In 1970, he sought the governorship of New York, but lost to Nelson A. Rockefeller (born 1908).

GOLDWATER, Barry Morris (born 1909). A Republican Senator from Arizona, Goldwater is one of the leaders of the conservative wing of his party. He was its candidate in the Presidential election of 1964 but was overwhelmingly defeated by **Lyndon B. Johnson** (*see*). Born in Phoenix, Goldwater attended the University of Arizona only one year, leaving to enter the family department-store business when his father died in 1929. He served in the U.S. Army Air Force during World War II and attained the rank of lieutenant colonel. Today, he is a major general in the air force reserve. Goldwater first entered politics in 1949, when he was elected to the Phoenix city council. Three years later he was elected to the

Senate, where he consistently championed states' rights and opposed the extension of federal control into social and economic spheres. Goldwater has advocated state right-to-work laws, the reduction of government ownership of utilities, and less spending for public-welfare programs and foreign aid. He has said that public-housing and urban-renewal programs should be managed by local authorities. A militant anti-Communist, Goldwater supported Senator **Joseph R. McCarthy** (*see*) of Wisconsin in his crusade against alleged Communist infiltration of the State Department. In 1957, Goldwater broke with the so-called modern Republicanism of President **Dwight D. Eisenhower** (*see*). His reelection to the Senate the following year, when the Democratic Party won a sweeping victory in Congressional elections, brought him to the forefront of national politics. Goldwater was nominated for the Presidency at the 1960 Republican National Convention but withdrew in favor of **Richard M. Nixon** (*see*). His victory at the Republican convention four years later caused a split within the party. In the ensuing campaign against Lyn-

NATIONAL REPUBLICAN HEADQUARTERS

Barry Goldwater

don Johnson, Goldwater's supporters coined the slogan "In your heart you know he's right." However, his dismissal of civil-rights issues, particularly those concerning Negroes, and his statement that he would, if necessary, use nuclear weapons in the event of war, turned many traditionally Republican voters against him. Goldwater received only 52 electoral votes, against 486 for Johnson. After four years in private life, Goldwater was reelected to the Senate in 1968. His publications include *Conscience of a Conservative* (1960), *Why Not Victory?* (1962), and *People and Places* (1967).

GULF OF TONKIN RESOLUTION. This controversial Congressional resolution, under which President **Lyndon B. Johnson** (*see*) derived the authority to greatly expand American involvement in the Vietnam war, was approved on August 7, 1964, by votes of 416 to 0 in the House of Representatives and 88 to 2 in the Senate. Specifically, it gave the President the authority "to take all necessary steps" to help any nation covered in the collective-security pact under which the eight-member **Southeast Asia Treaty Organization** (*see*) was created. Johnson sought the resolution following two attacks on American destroyers operating in the Gulf of Tonkin. On August 2, the Defense Department reported that three North Vietnamese torpedo boats had attacked the destroyer *Maddox* in international waters, 30 miles off the coast of North Vietnam. One torpedo boat was reportedly damaged by the *Maddox*'s guns and two others destroyed by fighter planes from the carrier *Ticonderoga*. Neither the *Maddox* nor the planes were damaged. Johnson responded to the incident by ordering another destroyer, the *C. Turner Joy,* to join the *Maddox* on patrol. Both were under orders to fight to destroy "any force which attacks them in international waters." On August 4, the Defense Department reported that the ships had been attacked by torpedo boats while 65 miles off North Vietnam. With the aid of carrier-based planes, the destroyers sank two boats without suffering any damage. In a nationwide television report shortly before midnight that same day, the President declared that the "repeated acts of violence against the armed forces of the United States must be met not only with alert defense but with positive reply." He announced that "air action" had already been carried out in retaliation against North Vietnamese gunboats and facilities. On August 5, Johnson sent Congress a special message asking its full support for any action to protect American forces. He had already received the backing of the Republican nominee in that year's Presidential election, **Barry Goldwater** *(see).* The only two Senators to vote against the resolution were Democrats Ernest Gruening (born 1887) of Alaska and Wayne Morse (born 1900) of Oregon. Morse argued that the resolution amounted to a "declaration of war" and was a part of an administrative plan to "escalate" the war in Vietnam. At the time of its approval, there were about 16,000 American "military advisers" in South Vietnam, aiding that government in its civil war against North Vietnam. American casualties totaled less than 200 dead and 2,000 wounded. Within four years, some 550,000 American troops were stationed in South Vietnam, and casualties amounted to more than 21,000 killed in action and 120,000 wounded. By then, Democratic Senator **J.**

William Fulbright *(see)* of Arkansas, chairman of the Foreign Relations Committee, had begun an inquiry into the events surrounding the attacks on the *Maddox* and the *C. Turner Joy.* Two questions were at issue: Did the Johnson administration react too hastily, and was there conclusive proof that the American destroyers had been attacked first and without cause? North Vietnam still maintained that the initial attack on the *Maddox* took place within its waters and that no later attack against the *Maddox* and the *C. Turner Joy* had ever occurred. Fulbright concluded that both ships had been engaged in spying operations and had violated North Vietnamese territorial waters at least once. After the captain who commanded both destroyers insisted that the ships had definitely been attacked on August 4 without provocation, Fulbright accused the Defense Department of intimidating military officers who wanted to offer testimony before his committee. He declared that Congress had approved the Gulf of Tonkin Resolution without full knowledge of what had occurred. Throughout the debate, the Johnson administration remained firm in its insistence that both attacks had been unprovoked and required retaliatory action. Replying to Fulbright's request in March, 1968, that the Foreign Relations Committee be informed before any further build-up of American forces in Vietnam, Secretary of State **Dean Rusk** *(see)* stated that the Gulf of Tonkin Resolution gave the administration Congressional endorsement of any action it might take and that advance consultations with Congress might provide valuable information to the enemy. Although the dispute was never settled, the adverse public reaction contributed to Johnson's

decision not to seek reelection in 1968 and his subsequent efforts to bring the North Vietnamese to the peace table. The Senate repealed the resolution in June, 1970.

H

HISS, Alger (born 1904). A high-ranking official in the State Department from 1936 to 1947, Hiss was the central figure in a sensational case of alleged espionage by agents of Communist Russia. Born in Baltimore, Hiss attended Johns Hopkins University, where he compiled an outstanding record of academic and extracurricular achievement before graduating in 1926. After obtaining a degree from the Harvard Law School in 1929, he served a year in Washington as secretary to Supreme Court Justice Oliver Wendell Holmes, Jr. (1841–1935). Hiss practiced law in Boston and New York from 1930 to 1933 and then began a successful governmental career in Washington. He was with the Agricultural Adjustment Administration (1933–1935) and the Department of Justice (1935–1936) before joining the State Department in 1936. Over the next decade, Hiss became a respected adviser on international matters to the State Department and the President. Considered one of the most capable of young New Deal officials, he accompanied President Franklin D. Roosevelt (1882–1945) to several important international meetings, including the Yalta Conference in 1945. Hiss also took an important part in the founding of the United Nations that year, serving as secretary general at the charter meeting of the U.N. in San Francisco. Hiss resigned from government service in 1947 to assume the presidency of the Carnegie Endow-

Alger Hiss

ment for International Peace. The following year, Whittaker Chambers (1901–1961), a magazine editor who claimed he had known Hiss in the 1930s when both were members of the Communist Party, told the House Committee on Un-American Activities that Hiss had stolen and handed over to him secret government documents. Representative **Richard M. Nixon** (*see*) of California was instrumental in investigating Chambers' allegations, all of which were denied by Hiss. Accused of lying under oath, Hiss was indicted in 1948 and brought to trial the following summer. After the jury failed to reach a verdict, a second trial was held. The evidence against Hiss was controversial. In addition, the jury heard Chambers described as a "psychopathic personality" and a chronic liar. Nevertheless, the jury found Hiss guilty on two counts of perjury in January, 1950. Hiss was

imprisoned until November, 1954. Three years later, he published *In the Court of Public Opinion,* in which he maintained his innocence. Hiss later entered business and engaged in lecturing and teaching in the New York area.

HOOVER, John Edgar (born 1895). The man who built the Federal Bureau of Investigation into one of the world's most effective law enforcement agencies, Hoover has headed the FBI for more than 45 years. During this time, the Director, as he prefers to be called, has been reappointed without regard to political party by every President. A native of Washington, D.C., Hoover worked by day as a messenger at the Library of Congress while attending night classes at George Washington University, from which he received his law degree in 1916. The following year, he passed the District of Columbia bar exam and went to work for the Department of Justice. After World War I, he became a special assistant to Attorney General A. Mitchell Palmer (1872–1936). At Palmer's request, Hoover organized and led a series of raids that resulted in the arrest and deportation of hundreds of alleged Communists and radical organizers. The operation was severely criticized as a flagrant violation of the Constitution's guarantee of due process. In 1921, Hoover became deputy director of the Justice Department's 13-year-old Bureau of Investigation. After the Teapot Dome Scandal in 1923 exposed widespread corruption in the bureau, Attorney General Harlan Fiske Stone (1872–1946) made Hoover the bureau's director. Hoover demanded and received the authority to fire corrupt officials within the agency. He eliminated political influence in appointments

and instituted a merit system for promotions. An innovative organizer, Hoover developed a central fingerprint file, a scientific crime laboratory, and a training academy for local police. He established high standards for FBI agents, recruiting only lawyers or accountants, and maintained a high level of discipline. His agents have no union and no tenure and can be transferred around the country at Hoover's direction. Initially, the bureau's activities were restricted to uncovering bank frauds and pursuing violators of the prostitution-curbing Mann Act. During Hoover's directorship, the FBI's criminal jurisdiction has expanded continuously. With the passage of the so-called Lindbergh Law in 1932, kidnapping became a federal offense, and the FBI has solved an incredible 99% of such crimes. Bank robbery also became a federal crime after it was discovered that bank robbers could evade capture by local police by crossing state lines. During the 1930s, FBI agents shot it out with such highly publicized bank robbers as John Dillinger (1904?–1934), Charles "Pretty Boy" Floyd (1907?–1934), Lester M. Gillis (alias "Baby Face" Nelson) (1909?–1934), and Arizona "Ma" Barker (?–1935). As World War II approached, the FBI turned its attention to national security. Within 72 hours of the Japanese attack on Pearl Harbor on December 7, 1941, the FBI had taken into custody 3,846 enemy aliens and seized large quantites of contraband armaments. During the war, the FBI made headlines with its quick seizure of eight German saboteurs, who were put ashore on Long Island and Florida from submarines. The bureau continued its spychasing activities into the 1950s, this time in pursuit of Communists. Amid the furor created by the anti-Communist investigations of Senator **Joseph R. McCarthy** (*see*), critics wondered if the FBI would not return to the high-handed practices of A. Mitchell Palmer. "The FBI," Hoover replied, "will always strive to preserve the civil liberties of every American citizen. We can never become . . . a Gestapo." In 1957, when a meeting of Mafia leaders in Apalachin, New York, received nationwide publicity, the FBI began to arm itself to fight organized crime. Four years later, Congress passed a law making it a federal crime to travel across state lines in order to violate gambling, extortion, or bribery laws. This put organized crime under the jurisdiction of the FBI. The bureau was at first structurally ill-adapted to enforce the new civil-rights laws enacted since 1954. The FBI has traditionally depended on the cooperation of local police —an arrangement that proved unworkable in the South in cases involving the rights of Negroes. However, by 1965, the FBI had developed a new information network in the South that enabled it to deal quickly and effectively with civil-rights violations. In 1964, President **Lyndon B. Johnson** (*see*) waived the mandatory retirement requirement on Hoover's 70th birthday, and he was reappointed to his post when President **Richard M. Nixon** (*see*) took office in 1969. A bachelor, Hoover lives in the modest Washington home where he was born. He does not participate in the social life of the nation's capital, although he is occasionally seen at baseball games and local racetracks.

HUMPHREY, Hubert Horatio, Jr. (born 1911). A Senator from Minnesota between 1949 and 1965 and Vice-President of the United States from 1965 to 1969, Humphrey was the Democratic candidate for President in the election of 1968. He and his running mate, Senator **Edmund S. Muskie** (*see*) of Maine, were narrowly defeated by Republicans **Richard M. Nixon** and **Spiro T. Agnew** (*see both*). Humphrey was born in Wallace, South Dakota. His father, a druggist, was a political liberal who schooled his son in the writings of Thomas Jefferson (1743–1826) and Thomas Paine (1737–1809). Humphrey grew up in Doland, South Dakota, where, known to his classmates as Pinky, he excelled academically and was an outstanding debator. He enrolled at the University of Minnestoa in 1929 but was forced to leave college after a year and a half to assist his father in his new drugstore in Huron, South Dakota, during the Depression years. In 1933, after attending the Denver School of Pharmacy, Humphrey became a registered pharmacist and managed the family business in South Dakota for the next several years while his father served in the state legislature. He returned to the University of Minnesota in 1937, graduating with honors two years later. He took a Master of Arts degree in political science at Louisiana State University in 1940. Ineligible for military service during World War II because of color blindness, Humphrey held various teaching and governmental positions in Minnesota between 1941 and 1943. Campaigning as a New Deal Democrat, he was defeated in the race for mayor of Minneapolis in 1943, but he was successful in his second bid for that office two years later. He was reelected in 1947 on the basis of his notable record as a municipal administrator and reformer. An early backer and member of the liberal Americans for Democratic Action, Humphrey was also a leader in combating Communist influence in Minnesota's new Democratic-Farmer-Labor Party. With the support of organized labor, Humphrey won election as Minnesota's first Democratic United States Senator in 1948. He was returned to office in 1954 and 1960. Humphrey soon became known as a champion of progressive social-welfare programs and other liberal-reform measures. He took the lead in advocating more federal action in the areas of urban renewal, housing, unemployment compensation, Social Security, minimum-wage laws, tax reform, conservation, aid to education, food-and-drug regulation, and assistance for small businesses. Although Humphrey's legislative abilities were recognized by his Senate colleagues, he alienated the powerful Southern conservative bloc by his crusading liberalism and his personal brashness. However, his friendship with Senate majority leader **Lyndon B. Johnson** (*see*) and the moderation of his oratorical aggressiveness gradually increased his popularity and power in the Senate. Elected "majority whip" (assistant majority leader) by his Democratic colleagues in 1961, Humphrey played a key role in obtaining ratification of the Nuclear Test Ban Treaty in 1963 and in securing passage of the Civil Rights Act of 1964. Humphrey campaigned for the Democratic nomination for President in 1960 but withdrew from the race after losing to **John F. Kennedy** (*see*) in the West Virginia primary. Selected by Johnson as his running mate in 1964, Humphrey became Vice-President after the Democrats' decisive victory in the November election. During the next four years, he presided over the Senate and represented the President in such areas as civil rights, space exploration, urban problems, and antipoverty programs. He also toured the Far East and spoke throughout the nation in defense of the Johnson administration's policy in Vietnam. After Johnson announced his retirement in 1968, Humphrey won his party's nomination for President despite bitter opposition from antiwar delegates at the Democratic National Convention in Chicago. Hampered by a lack of party unity and unwilling to renounce the unpopular foreign policies of the Johnson administration, Humphrey waged a strenuous but losing campaign for the Presidency, as Nixon polled about 500,000 more popular votes. He subsequently accepted a teaching position at Macalester College in Minnesota. He was re-elected to the Senate in 1970, taking the seat vacated by **Eugene J. McCarthy** (*see*).

J

JOHNSON, Lyndon Baines (born 1908). Johnson, who became the nation's 36th President after **John F. Kennedy** (*see*) was assassinated in 1963, rallied the American people at a time of despair but left office in 1969 with the nation deeply divided over the war in Vietnam. One of the most noted Senate majority leaders in American history, the tall, homespun Texan was born on a farm to a family referred to as a "stable of politicians." His father had served five terms in the Texas legislature, and his mother's ancestors included many distinguished officeholders. After working his way through Southwest Texas State Teachers College, Johnson graduated in 1930 and subsequently taught at a Houston high school. He entered politics in 1931 by working in the elec-

tion campaign of Representative Richard M. Kleberg (1887–1955) and subsequently became Kleberg's secretary in Washington, D.C. In 1934, "LBJ," as he was referred to, married Claudia Alta Taylor (born 1912), who had been nicknamed Lady Bird by her nursemaid. The couple had two daughters—Lynda Bird (born 1944) and Luci Baines (born 1947). Mrs. Johnson, who ably assisted her husband in his budding political career, developed the family farm and broadcasting enterprises into a multimillion-dollar empire. While in the nation's capital, Johnson became a friend of **Sam Rayburn** (*see*), a fellow Texan and friend of his father's who was rising to a position of influence in the House. In 1935, Rayburn persuaded President Franklin D. Roosevelt (1882–1945) to name Johnson the Texas director of the National Youth Administration. Johnson helped 30,000 youths find jobs or go to school, and he received a citation as the program's most outstanding director. In 1937, Johnson, running on a strong New Deal platform and supporting Roosevelt's scheme to pack the Supreme Court, defeated nine other candidates for a seat in the House of Representatives, and was reelected every two years through 1948. As a freshman Congressman, he was appointed to the prestigious Naval Affairs Committee. Early in World War II, Johnson, who was a member of the naval reserve, became the first Congressman to volunteer for active duty. He was sent to Australia and New Zealand, and later he received the Silver Star Medal for gallantry in action. In 1942, Johnson and other Congressmen were recalled to Washington by the President, who believed their services were of more value in Congress than on the war fronts. Although he won the Democratic

primary for the Senate in 1948, his 87-vote margin of victory was contested by his opponent, who obtained a court injunction to remove Johnson's name from the ballot. With the assistance of his friend and attorney, **Abe Fortas** (*see*), the case was taken to Supreme Court Justice Hugo Black (1886–1971), who ordered Johnson reinstated on the ballot. As a result, Johnson was elected to the first of two Senate terms (1949–1961). An astute politician, Johnson rose rapidly to influential positions in the Senate. He was chosen his party's whip in 1951 and the Democratic floor leader two years later. When the Democrats regained control of the Senate in 1955, Johnson became the youngest majority leader in the nation's history. As such, Johnson wielded great power and revealed his genius for persuasion and compromise. For the sake of national unity, he marshaled Democratic support behind the moderate programs of President **Dwight D. Eisenhower** (*see*), particularly in the field of foreign affairs. A skilled legislative craftsman, Johnson organized support for civil-rights bills in 1957 and 1960—the first such legislation since Reconstruction —and was also instrumental in the passage of the National Defense Education Act in 1958, as well as aid for depressed areas and health care for the aged. Although he suffered a serious heart attack in 1955, Johnson fully recovered, and in 1960 he decided to seek the Democratic Presidential nomination. He lost to Kennedy on the first ballot but accepted Kennedy's offer to run as Vice-President. Campaigning vigorously, Johnson helped to win the South for the Democratic Party. Under Kennedy, Johnson was kept well briefed on all policy matters. He presided over important Presidential committees on civil rights and space activities, was a member of the National Security Council, and was sent as Kennedy's emissary to 20 nations. He was thus the best-prepared Vice-President ever to inherit the Presidency when Kennedy was shot in Dallas on November 22, 1963. About an hour and a half after Kennedy's death, Johnson, who had been riding in the same motorcade three cars back, took the oath of office aboard the Presidential jet, Air Force One, at Love Field in Dallas. He immediately proclaimed a continuation of the late President's programs in civil-rights legislation, tax cuts, and foreign aid and, in a relatively short time, was able to get Congress to enact many measures that under Kennedy had seemed hopelessly stalled. In his first State of the Union message on January 8, 1964, Johnson announced a "war on poverty" and, later that spring, plans for a "Great Society." A master of the legislative process, Johnson, in his early months in office, obtained the passage of laws establishing Medicare, water-pollution controls, the Economic Opportunity Act, and a plan for model cities. A high point of his administration was the passage of the Civil Rights Act of 1964 (*see* **Civil-rights Movement**). In foreign policy, Johnson initially handled the explosive situation in Vietnam with restraint. On August 7, 1964, Congress passed the **Gulf of Tonkin Resolution** (*see*), authorizing him to "take all necessary steps, including the use of armed force," to aid the South Vietnamese government. In running for his first full term as President that fall, Johnson, misled by optimistic reports, stated that the South Vietnamese army could cope with the civil war there and pledged not to "supply American boys to do

World leaders try to fathom Johnson, an unknown commodity when he succeeded John F. Kennedy in 1963.

the job Asian boys should do." After defeating Republican **Barry Goldwater** (*see*) by nearly 16,000,000 votes—the largest majority in history—and winning 486 electoral votes to Goldwater's 52, Johnson ran into increasing criticism. Early in 1965, when South Vietnam seemed on the verge of falling to the Communists, Johnson ordered the bombing of North Vietnam and an escalation of the war. By the end of the year, the

number of American troops in Vietnam had climbed from about 23,000 to 184,000. A "credibility gap" was created during the 1965 crisis in the Dominican Republic. Attempting to explain why he sent 30,000 troops there, Johnson at first stated that the reason was to protect American lives. Later he said that it was to prevent a Communist takeover. The Vietnam war diverted Johnson's time and energy away from the Great Society programs, and Republican gains in the Congressional elections of 1966 precluded any chance of Johnson's fulfilling his domestic goals. By the end of 1967, there were more than 475,000 American soldiers in Vietnam (16,000 had by then been killed and 53,000 wounded), and there was no victory in sight. Costing the nation about $2,000,000,000 a month, the war produced a business slump. As criticism of his war policy became increasingly virulent, cities throughout the nation experienced antiwar demonstrations and race riots. Crime and violence became national issues, and Johnson was uncertain as to how to respond to Negro demands for immediate equality in schools, housing, and jobs. Because he had long sought to govern by consensus and was always conscious of his own popularity (he kept the results of public-opinion polls in his jacket pockets), Johnson called a halt in the bombing of North Vietnam after Senator **Eugene J. McCarthy** (*see*) of Minnesota, a peace advocate, won an impressive 42.2% of the vote in the first 1968 Democratic Presidential primary in New Hampshire in March. Johnson also announced that he would not seek another term. After he left office the following January, he retired to his Texas ranch and began work on his memoirs, proceeds from which will go to a foundation in Austin.

K

KENNEDY, Edward Moore (born 1932). The youngest of the nine children of financier and former Ambassador to Great Britain Joseph P. Kennedy (1888–1969), "Ted" Kennedy was catapulted into the national political limelight after the assassinations of his brothers **John F. Kennedy** and **Robert F. Kennedy** (*see both*). His future in politics, however, was clouded by an incident in July, 1969, when he was involved in the drowning of Mary Jo Kopechne (1941–1969), a friend of the Kennedy family. Born in Brookline, Massachusetts, Ted Kennedy attended school in England while his father was ambassador there (1938–1940). He entered Har-

vard in 1950. In the spring of his freshman year, Kennedy was suspended from school after it was discovered that a friend had taken a Spanish examination for him. He then joined the army and served two years in Europe as a private. Reentering Harvard in 1953, Kennedy did well in public speaking, history, and government and played first-string end on the football team. Turned down by Harvard Law School after his graduation in 1956, Kennedy spent a year at the International Law Institute at The Hague, in the Netherlands, before entering the University of Virginia Law School. He received his degree in 1959 and, that November, married the former Joan Bennett Wiggin (born 1936). Kennedy's first experience in politics had come

in 1958 when he served as campaign manager for his brother John, who was then seeking a second term in the Senate. In 1960, Ted Kennedy coordinated the Western states in his brother's bids for the Democratic Presidential nomination and the election itself. Afterward, he took a position as an assistant to the district attorney in Suffolk County, Massachusetts, and also traveled extensively. In March, 1962, Kennedy announced his intention to run for the Senate seat formerly held by John. The announcement by the 30-year-old brother of the President was greeted with opposition by most Republicans and many liberals. In the primary contest, Kennedy was pitted against Edward J. McCormack, Jr. (born 1923), the state attorney general and the

UPI

The Kennedy family posed a few days after John was elected President. Seated, left to right, are his sister Mrs. R. Sargent Shriver, his parents Mr. and Mrs. Joseph Kennedy, his wife Jacqueline, and brother Edward. Standing are Mrs. Robert F. Kennedy, brother-in-law Stephen Smith, Mrs. Smith, the President-elect, Robert Kennedy, sister Mrs. Peter Lawford, brother-in-law R. Sargent Shriver, Mrs. Edward Kennedy, and brother-in-law Peter Lawford.

nephew of then Speaker of the House John W. McCormack (born 1891). Kennedy was attacked as an immature, unqualified opportunist, but he won 69% of the vote in the primary and went on to defeat Republican George Cabot Lodge (born 1927). As a freshman legislator, Kennedy worked quietly and diligently, carefully observing Senate traditions. Both John Kennedy and **Lyndon B. Johnson** (*see*) judged him the best politician in the family. In 1964, Ted Kennedy was reelected to a full term by the greatest margin in Massachusetts' history—more than 1,100,000 votes. At the time, he was recovering from a nearly fatal private-plane crash that had taken place in June, near fogbound Westfield, Massachusetts. He suffered fractures of his spine in six places and two broken ribs and was hospitalized for 180 days. Kennedy recovered in time to take his Senate seat in January, 1965. In his first speech after the slaying of his brother Robert in Los Angeles on June 5, 1968, Ted Kennedy said, "I pick up a fallen standard . . . . I shall try to carry forward that special commitment to justice, to excellence, to courage that distinguished their lives." At the Democratic National Convention that August, there was talk of placing Kennedy's name in nomination, but he discouraged it. In January, 1969, however, Kennedy was elected Senate whip, defeating Russell B. Long (born 1918) of Louisiana in a test of political strength that many believed was the first step in his seeking the Presidency in 1972. On July 18, Kennedy attended a party on Chappaquiddick Island near Edgartown, Massachusetts. Five other men and six women—all campaign workers for Robert Kennedy or friends of the Kennedy family—also attended. The next day, one of the

women, Miss Kopechne, was found drowned. Kennedy pleaded guilty to the charge of leaving the scene of the accident. He explained to a nationwide television audience that he had left the party with Miss Kopechne and had driven off a narrow wooden bridge. He admitted waiting nearly nine hours to report the accident to the police. Kennedy termed his leaving the accident "indefensible" and asked Massachusetts residents to help him decide whether to remain in office. Letters and telegrams supported him overwhelmingly. On July 30, he announced that he would seek reelection in 1970 but ruled out any Presidential possibilities in 1972. Although no indictment was ever handed down in the Chappaquiddick case, the release of the transcript of the hearings into it disclosed that the presiding judge believed Kennedy had been negligent in his driving and questioned the truth of the Senator's testimony. He won re-election handily but later lost the post of Senate whip.

KENNEDY, John Fitzgerald (1917–1963). The 35th President of the United States and the first Roman Catholic to be Chief Executive, Kennedy—who was only 43 when elected—brought a youthful exuberance and a new emphasis on the arts to the White House. He had passed crucial tests in foreign relations and was attempting to implement a far-reaching domestic program when he was assassinated by a deranged young man on November 22, 1963, in Dallas, Texas. Kennedy was born in Brookline, Massachusetts, the second son of financier and diplomat Joseph P. Kennedy (1888–1969). In 1938, he left Harvard in his junior year to travel to Europe and work as a secretary to his father, who had been appointed

ambassador to Great Britain. Kennedy used his European experience to advantage in writing his undergraduate thesis, later published as *Why England Slept* (1940). He graduated cum laude in 1940 and became an ensign in the naval reserves in October, 1941. After the Japanese attack on Pearl Harbor on December 7, 1941, Kennedy immediately requested sea duty and, after further training, was assigned in April, 1943, to the South Pacific. On August 2, Kennedy's torpedo boat, the *PT-109,* was rammed and sunk by a Japanese destroyer. Kennedy ordered his men to swim the three miles to shore, and he himself towed a wounded crew member. Aided by friendly natives, the men were rescued, and Kennedy received several medals for bravery. Four months later, he returned to a hospital near his home to recuperate from malaria and to receive treatment for a recurrent back injury. While in the hospital, Kennedy learned that his older brother, Joseph P. Kennedy, Jr. (1915–1944), had been killed while on an air mission over the English Channel. Later, Kennedy was to say, "Just as I went into politics when Joe died, if anything happened to me tomorrow my brother Bobby would run for my seat in the Senate. And if Bobby died, Teddy would take over for him" (*see* **Kennedy, Robert F.** and **Kennedy, Edward M.**). After the war, John worked briefly as a journalist for Hearst's International News Service before running as a Democrat for the House of Representatives. With help from his entire family and navy friends, Kennedy won convincingly and was twice reelected (1947–1953). As a Representative, he generally supported the domestic programs of President **Harry S. Truman** (*see*) but was occasionally critical of foreign policy, particularly with regard to the Far East. In April, 1952, Kennedy announced he would run for the Senate, opposing incumbent Henry Cabot Lodge, Jr. (born 1902). He beat Lodge by 70,000 votes, though the Republican Presidential candidate, **Dwight D. Eisenhower** (*see*), carried Massachusetts by more than 200,000 votes. During his first Senate term, Kennedy required two back operations, and while recuperating, he wrote the Pulitzer Prize-winning *Profiles in Courage* (1956), which included portraits of political leaders who defied public opinion to take a stand on what they believed was right. Kennedy made a bid for the Democratic Vice-Presidential nomination in 1956 after the party's Presidential candidate, **Adlai E. Stevenson** (*see*), threw the nomination open to the convention. However, he lost on the third ballot to Estes Kefauver (1903–1963) of Tennessee. Two years later, Kennedy won re-election to the Senate by nearly 900,000 votes. Kennedy decided to seek the Presidency in January, 1960, and declared his intention to test his vote-getting power in the Democratic primaries. He won easily in New Hampshire, but the key tests were in Wisconsin, where **Hubert H. Humphrey** (*see*) was popular, and West Virginia, where Kennedy's religion and wealth were considered drawbacks. Nevertheless, Kennedy captured 56% of the vote in Wisconsin and 61% in West Virginia. His nomination at the Democratic National Convention that July came on the first ballot. His chief rival, **Lyndon B. Johnson** (*see*), was chosen as his running mate to give balance to the ticket. In his acceptance speech, Kennedy pledged to explore a New Frontier, which he defined as "uncharted areas

of science and space, unsolved problems of peace and war, unconquered pockets of ignorance and prejudice, unanswered questions of poverty and surplus." Most political observers agreed that the turning point of the campaign was a series of four televised debates between Kennedy and the Republican nominee, **Richard M. Nixon** (*see*). Kennedy appeared handsome, relaxed, and confident, while Nixon appeared in need of a shave, tired, and uncertain. Kennedy won the election by a narrow margin—just a little over 100,000 votes out of nearly 69,000,000 cast. He won 303 electoral votes to Nixon's 219. At Kennedy's inauguration, **Robert Frost** (*see*) recited one of his poems, and the new President, in his own address, declared, "And so, my fellow Americans: ask not what your country can do for you—ask what you can do for your country." Kennedy gathered a group of young, intelligent aides to assist him in carrying out his programs. Among them were his younger brother Robert F. Kennedy, who was appointed Attorney General; Pierre Salinger (born 1925), who became his press secretary; Robert Sargent Shriver, Jr. (born 1915), a brother-in-law who was named to head the newly created Peace Corps; Theodore C. Sorensen (born 1928), the President's major speech writer; and Arthur M. Schlesinger, Jr. (born 1917), a historian who became a special assistant to the President. Kennedy was initially occupied with a series of international crises. The **Bay of Pigs invasion** (see) of Cuba in April, 1961, which had been planned by the Eisenhower administration and endorsed by military and intelligence men in Kennedy's, proved a fiasco. Next, a Communist take-over threatened Laos. Ken-

nedy considered intervention but settled for an international conference guaranteeing Laotian neutrality. However, he slowly increased military aid to South Vietnam and, at the time of his death, about 16,000 American troops and "advisers" were stationed there. In June, 1961, Kennedy met with Russian Premier Nikita Khrushchev (born 1894) in Vienna, but they were unable to reach any agreement. In August, the East Germans built the Berlin Wall, sealing off West Berlin. Two years later, Kennedy underscored American support of West Germany when he told a crowd assembled at the wall, "*Ich bin ein Berliner* (I am a Berliner)." Earlier, in October, 1962, Kennedy faced the gravest crisis of the cold war when he learned that Russia was installing offensive missiles in Cuba. After days of high-level meetings, Kennedy ruled out both an air strike and passive acceptance of the Russian challenge. He decided to impose a naval quarantine of the island, with a pledge that America would not invade if the Russians agreed to halt further missile delivery and to dismantle the ones that were there. A nuclear war was avoided when Khrushchev agreed to Kennedy's terms. The following year, a nuclear test ban treaty was concluded with Russia, Great Britain, and more than 100 other nations. A two-way telegraph-teleprinter line—the "hot line"—was installed in the summer of 1963 to provide instant communications between the White House and the Kremlin in Moscow. In addition, Kennedy established the Peace Corps, which sent young Americans to help underdeveloped nations throughout the world, and the Alliance for Progress, to aid Latin America. His most persistent domestic problem was civil rights (*see* **Civil-rights**

Movement). Although he waited 22 months to sign an executive order ending racial discrimination in federal housing, he sent federal marshals to enforce integration at the University of Mississippi and the desegregation of shops and restaurants in Birmingham, Alabama. Kennedy also gave his endorsement to the March on Washington in August, 1963, a peaceful rights demonstration led by **Martin Luther King, Jr.** (*see*), and pressed for the passage of the most comprehensive civil-rights bill in the nation's history. However, the bill and most of Kennedy's other domestic legislation were stalled in Congress at the time of his death. As 1963 neared an end, Kennedy began to mend Democratic political fences in preparation for seeking reelection in 1964. He decided to visit Texas to unite the warring party factions there. He was shot by Lee Harvey Oswald (1939–1963) while riding in an open limousine through downtown Dallas with his wife, Jacqueline (born 1929), and the governor of Texas, John B. Connally (born 1917), and his wife. The President was shot at 12:30 P.M. and pronounced dead at 1:00 P.M. at nearby Parkland Hospital. Vice-President Johnson, who had been riding in the third car behind Kennedy's in the motorcade, was sworn in as President at 2:39 P.M. aboard Air Force One at Dallas' Love Field. Kennedy's body was flown to Washington, where it lay in state for two days at the Capitol Rotunda. He was buried on November 25 in Arlington National Cemetery after a funeral attended by many world leaders and watched by millions on television. The day before his funeral, Oswald, who had been involved in various extreme groups, was shot by Dallas nightclub owner Jack Ruby (1911–1967), while being trans-

ferred to another jail. Millions of television viewers watched the incident in horror. Ruby was arrested, tried, convicted, and sentenced to death. The conviction was reversed by a Texas court of appeals, but Ruby died of cancer in January, 1967, while awaiting a retrial. After Kennedy's assassination, rumors spread that Oswald might have had accomplices or that a conspiracy was involved. However, a special commission, headed by Chief Justice **Earl Warren** (*see*), concluded after taking testimony from 552 witnesses that Oswald had acted alone.

KENNEDY, Robert Francis (1925–1968). Considered a champion of civil rights and peace in Vietnam by his followers, but a cold-blooded, ruthless, power-hungry opportunist by his enemies, Kennedy was assassinated in June, 1968, after winning the California Democratic Presidential primary. The seventh child of Joseph P. Kennedy (1888–1969), "Bobby" was a sophomore at Harvard when his oldest brother, Joseph, Jr. (1915–1944), was killed in a plane crash over the English Channel during World War II. Kennedy left Harvard and enlisted as a seaman second class on a destroyer named for his brother. He returned to Harvard after the war in 1946 and, despite the fact that he was only 5 feet 9 inches and weighed less than 160 pounds, won a letter in football before his graduation in 1948. He spent that summer in Palestine covering the war for the Boston *Post*. That fall, he entered the law school at the University of Virginia. His first job after graduation in 1951 was with the Justice Department's Internal Security Division. He resigned the following year to manage the senatorial campaign

of his brother **John F. Kennedy** (*see*) and first gained his reputation as a "fresh kid." After his brother's election, Robert Kennedy became assistant counsel on the Permanent Investigations Subcommittee headed by **Joseph R. McCarthy** (*see*) of Wisconsin. He resigned six months later after clashes with the panel's head counsel, Roy Cohn (born 1927), but he never repudiated McCarthy for his Communist witch-hunt. After managing John's unsuccessful bid for the Vice-Presidential nomination in 1956, Robert became the chief counsel on the Senate Labor Rackets Committee investigating improper activities in the labor-management field. His first target was Dave Beck (born 1894), president of the International Brotherhood of Teamsters, who was convicted of grand larceny and income-tax evasion. Beck's successor, James R. Hoffa (born 1913), proved a more formidable foe. Hoffa referred to Kennedy as a "young, dim-witted, curly-headed smart aleck." Kennedy vowed to jump off the Capitol dome if he failed to secure a conviction. When Hoffa was acquitted, his lawyer offered Kennedy a parachute. Kennedy resigned from the committee in 1959 to write *The Enemy Within,* a description of his Teamster investigations, and to start the groundwork for his brother's Presidential bid in 1960. Kennedy supervised the campaign organization. After his brother won the nomination, Robert was sent to offer the Vice-Presidential nomination to **Lyndon B. Johnson** (*see*). He made it clear to Johnson that he disapproved of the move, and the two were bitter rivals from that point on. In late October, during the election campaign, Robert asked a judge to set bail for **Martin Luther King, Jr.** (*see*), who was in a Georgia jail following a civil-rights demonstration—a move that swung many Negro votes to Kennedy. After the election, despite charges of nepotism, President Kennedy appointed his brother Attorney General. Robert also became his brother's most trusted adviser. He reorganized the Justice Department and began an all-out attack on organized crime and racketeering, and, once again, Hoffa. Hoffa finally went to jail in 1967 for jury tampering and diverting union funds. Kennedy also took a firm position on civil rights. He increased the number of Negro lawyers in the Justice Department from 10 to 50, enforced school desegregation guidelines, and used federal troops to force desegregation of shops and restaurants in Birmingham, Alabama, in May, 1963. Kennedy supported his brother's stance against Russian Premier Nikita Khrushchev (born 1894) in the Cuban missile crisis in 1962. *Thirteen Days* (1969), a book about the crisis by Kennedy, was published posthumously. After John was assassinated on November 22, 1963, Kennedy stayed on as Attorney General, but his zeal was gone. Slowly, he began to reenter public life. However, in July, 1964, Johnson, now the President, ruled out Kennedy as his Vice-Presidential choice in that year's elections. A few weeks later, Kennedy changed his residency to Long Island and announced that he would run for the Senate from New York. Overcoming accusations of carpetbagging, he defeated incumbent Senator Kenneth B. Keating (born 1900), a Republican liberal, by more than 700,000 votes. The Kennedy family thus became the first in history to send three brothers to the Senate. Unlike most freshman Senators, Kennedy immediately began to assert himself. In

1965, he sponsored major amendments to bills on school aid, the poverty drive, voting rights, and foreign aid. He concentrated on problems of minority groups and increasingly moved away from Johnson's policy of escalation in the Vietnam war. Shortly after Senator **Eugene J. McCarthy** (*see*), a peace advocate, won 42.2% of the vote in the New Hampshire primary in March, 1968, Kennedy announced his own candidacy. Although accused of ruthless opportunism for having waited so long, Kennedy won the Indiana primary and then the Nebraska primary. However, he lost to McCarthy in Oregon— the first loss by any Kennedy in 27 primary and election contests. On June 4, Kennedy won the California primary, his most important victory. Following a victory speech that night, he was walking through the kitchen of the Ambassador Hotel in Los Angeles when he was shot by Sirhan Sirhan (born 1944), a Jordanian who objected to Kennedy's pro-Israel statements. A day later, Kennedy died. Hundreds of thousands of people filed past his casket in St. Patrick's Cathedral in New York, where his funeral services were held. Senator **Edward M. Kennedy** (*see*), who delivered the eulogy, declared, "My brother need not be idealized or enlarged in death beyond what he was in life, to be remembered simply as a good and decent man who saw wrong and tried to right it, saw suffering and tried to heal it, saw war and tried to stop it." A train carried Kennedy's body to Washington, where he was buried near his brother John in Arlington National Cemetery. Sirhan was indicted for first-degree murder, convicted, and sentenced to die in the California gas chamber. His attorneys have appealed for a new trial.

KING, Martin Luther, Jr. (1929–1968). The foremost civil-rights leader of his time, King sought full freedom and equality for the American Negro. The winner of the 1964 Nobel Peace Prize for his nonviolent approach to social change, he was assassinated while in Memphis, Tennessee, to lead a protest strike by city garbage workers. The son of a Baptist minister, King grew up in Atlanta, Georgia, and attended Morehouse College. While there, he read the essay *On Civil Disobedience* by Henry David Thoreau (1817–1862) and became a dedicated advocate of the concept of nonviolent resistance as a way to bring about social changes. Later, he attributed his nonviolent philosophy to the teachings of Jesus Christ and the famous Indian leader Mahatma Gandhi (1869–1948) as well. After earning his doctorate in systematic theology from Boston University in 1955, King became pastor of a Negro Baptist church in Montgomery, Alabama. Here, his first nonviolent struggle for human rights took place in December, 1955, when he organized and led Montgomery's Negroes in a boycott of the city's racially segregated bus lines. As King pointed out, the conflict was "not between white people and Negro people," but "between justice and injustice." During the nearly year-long boycott, the bus company lost 65% of its business. After the Supreme Court ruled racial discrimination on public buses unconstitutional in November, 1956, Montgomery integrated its buses. King then carried his crusade to other parts of the South. He helped to form and headed the Southern Christian Leadership Conference (S.C.L.C.) to implement federal civil-rights laws and to promote nationwide understand-

Dr. Martin Luther King, Jr., receives the Nobel Peace Prize in 1964.

ing of the plight of the Negro. In 1961, King started a lunch-counter "sit-in" campaign to protest segregation in Southern chain stores. He also participated in "freedom rides" to test segregation on buses operating between states. In his quest for civil rights, King was frequently involved in legal action, jailed, or threatened with violence by white extremists. He ignored personal danger, saying, "It may get me crucified. I may even die. But I want it said even if I die in the struggle that 'He died to make me free.'" In April, 1963, King began a campaign to end discrimination in all areas of public life in Birmingham, Alabama—the most segregated city of the South. The city's commissioner of public safety, Eugene "Bull" Connor (born 1917), attacked demonstrators with high-pressure fire hoses and trained dogs, arrested approximately 3,300 people, and put King in prison, at one point in solitary confinement, for eight days. However, Birmingham officials eventually acceded to King's demands for a program of desegregation, and he emerged as an acknowledged leader of the

Civil-rights Movement (*see*) in the United States. Nearly 800 similar demonstrations were staged in cities of the North and the South. In the summer of 1963, King helped to organize the Freedom March of both Negroes and whites to Washington, D.C. Speaking on the steps of the Lincoln Memorial before a crowd of more than 200,000 people on August 28, King declared, "I have a dream that my four little children will one day live in a nation where they will not be judged by the color of their skins, but by the content of their character." In 1965, King sponsored voter-registration drives for Southern Negroes. He cooperated at first with President Lyndon B. Johnson (*see*) but later criticized his conduct of the Vietnam war, which King believed was being fought at the expense of pressing domestic needs. When, in 1966, several civil-rights groups embraced the militant philosophy of "black power" and repudiated integration with whites, King disassociated himself from them. He blamed such extremists for the wave of riots that swept the nation in the summer of 1967. On

April 3, 1968, King arrived in Memphis to organize support for 1,300 striking sanitation workers. That night, before a crowd of followers, King cited recent threats on his life but shrugged them off saying, "It really doesn't matter what happens now. Because I've been to the mountaintop . . . . And I've looked over, and I've seen the promised land." The next day, as King was standing on his motel-room balcony, he was killed by an assassin's bullet. Several months later, a white suspect named James Earl Ray (born 1928) was apprehended for the murder in London and extradited. On March 11, 1969, Ray pleaded guilty to slaying King and was sentenced to 99 years' imprisonment in the Tennessee State Prison at Nashville. King's widow, Coretta Scott King (born 1927), and his closest friend, the Reverend Dr. Ralph Abernathy (born 1926), have since carried on King's work.

M

McCARTHY, Eugene Joseph (born 1916). An outspoken opponent of the Vietnam war, McCarthy, with the aid of thousands of young amateur followers, won an unexpected 42.2% of the vote in the 1968 New Hampshire primary. His strong showing was instrumental in the decision of President **Lyndon B. Johnson** (*see*) not to seek reelection. Although he was subsequently defeated for the party's Presidential nomination by **Hubert H. Humphrey** (*see*) at the riot-torn Democratic National Convention that August, McCarthy inspired a reappraisal of U.S. policy in Southeast Asia that led to preliminary peace talks in Paris. Of Irish-German descent, McCarthy was born in a farm hamlet in Minnesota. He graduated from Saint John's University in Minnesota at the age of 19 in 1935 and received a master's degree from the University of Minnesota four years later. McCarthy taught social science in public schools in the state until 1940, when he became a professor of economics at Saint John's. During World War II, he served as a civilian technical adviser to the War Department's intelligence division from 1942 to 1945 and, after a year of teaching high school, was appointed acting chairman of the sociology department at the College of Saint Thomas in St. Paul. While at Saint Thomas in 1948, McCarthy helped Humphrey, a fellow Minnesotan, take command of the newly merged Democratic-Farmer-Labor Party. McCarthy ran for the House of Representatives that same year and was elected to the first of five terms (1949–1959). He won reelection to his third term by 37,000 votes in 1952, despite being "smeared" as a pro-Communist after he debated Republican Senator **Joseph R. McCarthy** (*see*) of Wisconsin, who was then engaged in a witch-hunt into alleged Communist infiltration of the State Department. While in the House in the 1950s, "Gene" McCarthy, who often wrote poetry and essays, formed a liberal discussion group that became known as McCarthy's Mavericks and was later reorganized into the Democratic Study Group. He was first elected to the Senate in 1959 and was reelected six years later. McCarthy took no firm stand on the Vietnam war until January, 1966, when he joined 14 other Senators in appealing to President Johnson to extend a temporary pause in the bombing of North Vietnam as a way of showing America's sincerity in wanting to end the war. When

Eugene J. McCarthy

Johnson reinstituted the bombing, McCarthy became a critic of American policy. That August, after hearing Undersecretary of State Nicholas deB. Katzenbach (born 1922) say that the President did not need any Congressional declaration to conduct the war, McCarthy vowed, "There is only one thing to do —take it to the country." Although a lackluster campaigner who sprinkled his speeches with erudition and caustic wit, McCarthy attracted thousands of young people to his drive for the Presidential nomination. Many from across the nation traveled to New Hampshire in March, 1968, to ring doorbells for him. Insisting that the war symbolized a moral crisis in the nation, McCarthy said, "The great issue in this contest between President Johnson and myself is not Vietnam. It is not rising violence in the cities or rising prices. It is one of leadership and the direction of our nation." Although opinion polls before the primary showed McCarthy getting only 10 to 20% of the vote, he polled

42.2% to Johnson's 49.4%. Counting the more than 5,500 Republicans who wrote in McCarthy's name on their party's ballot, he trailed the President by only 230 votes. Almost immediately following the primary, Senator **Robert F. Kennedy** (*see*) of New York, another antiwar advocate, announced his candidacy. Thus imperiled within his own party, Johnson dropped his plans to run again and decided to devote himself to furthering peace negotiations. With Johnson's support, Vice-President Humphrey then announced his own candidacy for the Democratic nomination. A late starter, he did not take part in the final primaries but concentrated instead on gathering regular party support. When Kennedy was assassinated hours after winning the California primary on June 5, McCarthy failed to win over his backers. The outbreak of violence between antiwar demonstrators and the Chicago police at the Democratic National Convention that August embittered McCarthy, and he refused to appear on the convention platform with Humphrey, the winner. He later announced that he would not seek reelection as a Democrat and, to the amazement of liberal supporters, resigned his membership on the Senate Foreign Relations Committee to allow the seating of a prowar Senator. His book describing the 1968 Presidential elections, *The Year of the People,* was published in 1969.

McCARTHY, Joseph Raymond (1909–1957). This Republican Senator from Wisconsin gave his name to the practice of making unsubstantiated accusations of disloyalty and using unfair methods of investigations— McCarthyism. The center of bitter controversy during the early 1950s after he charged that several government agencies and the army harbored hundreds of Communists, "Communist-sympathizers," and espionage agents, he was censured by the Senate for numerous abuses, including contempt. McCarthy was born on a farm near Appleton, Wisconsin. After attending country schools, he enrolled in 1930 at Marquette University in Milwaukee, where he studied law. Admitted to the Wisconsin bar in 1935, McCarthy was soon involved in local politics in Shawano County, first as a Democrat and then as a Republican. In 1939, he was elected to a circuit-court judgeship in Wisconsin. "Young Judge Joe," as he called himself, was soon widely known for his informal and lively manner of holding court. Commissioned a lieutenant in the Marine Corps in 1942, he served as an intelligence officer in the Pacific Theater, winning promotion to captain. While still on active duty, he returned to Wisconsin in 1944 to campaign —in uniform—for the Republican nomination for the Senate but was defeated in the primary election. McCarthy resumed his judicial post after resigning his commission in 1945. The following year, he won the Republican nomination for the Senate over the liberal incumbent, Robert M. LaFollette, Jr. (1895–1953), who had recently switched from the Progressive Party to the Republican ranks. McCarthy then easily defeated his Democratic opponent in November. He had barely reached Washington, D.C., to take his seat when he initiated a controversy with John L. Lewis (1880–1969), president of the United Mine Workers Union, which was then on strike. McCarthy suggested that striking miners be drafted into the army. In February, 1950, in a speech at Wheeling, West Virginia, McCarthy charged

that there were 205 "known Communists" in the State Department, then headed by **Dean Acheson** (*see*). Following several similar speeches, McCarthy was called before a special subcommittee of the Senate Foreign Relations Committee headed by Millard E. Tydings (1890–1961) of Maryland and asked to substantiate his charges. This was the first of five investigations that McCarthy was to undergo in the next four years during what is now widely regarded as a "witch-hunt" that cost many citizens their reputations and their jobs. After extensive testimony, during which McCarthy was unable to identify a single Communist in the State Department, the committee issued a report that accused him of perpetrating "a fraud and a hoax" and termed his accusations "irresponsible" and "untruthful." Later in 1950, after Tydings was defeated for reelection in Maryland, an investigation by the Senate Committee on Privileges and Elections found that McCarthy and his supporters had helped to engineer Tydings' defeat in a "despicable 'back street' type of campaign." Undeterred, McCarthy, who became chairman of the Senate Committee on Government Operations in 1951, launched an attack on the Democratic administrations of Presidents Franklin D. Roosevelt (1882–1945) and **Harry S. Truman** (*see*), terming them "twenty years of treason." McCarthy soon came into conflict with **Dwight D. Eisenhower,** then head of the military forces of the **North Atlantic Treaty Organization** (*see both*), when he questioned the loyalty of Eisenhower's former army superior, General George C. Marshall (1880–1959). In the fall of 1951, a special Senate subcommittee was formed to investigate Senator McCarthy's financial affairs. However, Mc-

Carthy refused to testify. One point at issue was a $10,000 check. He had received it from a company that had gotten $37,-500,000 from a federal agency that a committee he served on had jurisdiction over. He contended that the check was for a pamphlet he had written. Re-elected to the Senate after a strenuous campaign fight in 1952, McCarthy returned to the attack in 1953, assailing—without result—several of President Eisenhower's diplomatic appointees. The Eisenhower administration was soon included in McCarthy's "treason" charge, and McCarthy found himself excluded from White House social functions. In 1953, McCarthy, as chairman of the Permanent Subcommittee on Investigations, began probing alleged "security risks" in the State Department's Voice of America and the army. The famous Army-McCarthy hearings occurred in April and May of 1954. McCarthy charged that "subversives" were knowingly employed at various military installations. The army countered by alleging that McCarthy had tried to secure preferential treatment for a former staff aide, then in service. Several military men were mercilessly cross-examined and subjected to insult by the McCarthy staff. The 26-day hearings, nationally televised, produced much sensation but little substance. The following December, the Senate voted to "condemn" McCarthy for his contemptuous and abusive conduct. This censure, combined with Democratic control of Congress after the 1954 elections, quickly reduced McCarthy's influence. His health declined rapidly, and three years later he died of acute hepatitis.

MALCOLM X (1925–1965). Malcolm X was one of the most

Malcolm X

influential black-nationalist leaders of the 1950s and '60s. He was a leading member of the Nation of Islam (Black Muslims) for nearly 10 years before breaking away to found the Muslim Mosque, Inc., and the Organization for Afro-American Unity a year before he was shot to death. Malcolm X was born Malcolm Little in Omaha, Nebraska. His father was a black clergyman who supported the "back-to-Africa" movement begun by the Jamaican Negro Marcus Garvey (1887–1940) in the early 20th century. Malcolm's reddish-brown hair and light complexion testified to the fact that his maternal grandfather was white—a heritage that Malcolm acknowledged with bitterness. The 11 children of the Little family moved with their parents to Lansing, Michigan, where their home was burned by white racists when Malcolm was four years old. Two years later, his father was killed by a streetcar in an apparent accident, though Malcolm believed that he had been murdered. Several years later, the family was forced to break up, and Malcolm was sent to a public institution. The only black youth in his school in Mason, Michigan, Malcolm was an outstanding student. However, he left after the eighth grade to live with a sister in Boston. There, and later in New York City, where he worked as a waiter in a Harlem nightclub, he engaged in numerous illegal activities. Known as Big Red because of his height and coloring, he sold drugs, worked as a procurer, and became involved in gambling rackets. After he began using cocaine, Malcolm turned to burglary to support his habit. He was arrested in Boston and sentenced to the state prison at Charlestown in 1946, before his 21st birthday. After hearing from his brothers and sisters of a new black-centered religion, Malcolm began to correspond from his prison cell with Elijah Muhammed (born 1897), the founder of the Nation of Islam, whose beliefs are modeled after the Moslem religion. Elijah Muhammed taught that the black man was the first human inhabitant of the earth and was superior to the "white devils" who came later. After serving a seven-year prison term, Malcolm went to Muslim headquarters in Chicago to join the movement. He ceased using the surname of Little, believing it to have been the name of whites who had enslaved his forebears. Instead he gave his last name as X. He also abandoned what he described as the vices of the white Christian world and embraced the strict Black Muslim discipline. Malcolm's commanding personality, intelligence, and speaking abilities soon made him an important figure in the Muslim organization. After touring the nation to enlist support for it, he was placed in charge of Mosque No. 7 in New York, where he rapidly built up the membership and resources of the Mosque. Malcolm was married to a fellow Muslim, Sister Betty X, in 1958. They had four children. Shortly after the assassination of President **John F. Kennedy** (*see*) on November 22, 1963, Malcolm was suspended by Elijah Muhammed for saying that the slaying was an instance of "chickens coming home to roost" (his remark apparently meant that the white man's violence had now turned against himself). The rift between the Muslim leaders was never repaired, and in March, 1964, Malcolm founded his independent Muslim Mosque in New York. Three months later, he established the nonreligious Organization for Afro-American Unity. Unlike the Black Muslims, its aim was to seek black equality without separating from the white community. Throughout 1964, Malcolm, in addition to holding numerous rallies in New York to build support for his new group, conducted speaking tours throughout the United States. He also traveled to Europe, the Middle East, and Asia. Malcolm gradually modified his uncompromising black racism to advocate the brotherhood of all races. In mid-February, 1965, Malcolm's home in the Queens borough of New York was destroyed by fire bombs. He alleged that this was an assassination attempt by agents of Elijah Muhammed. The next Sunday, February 21, while addressing a meeting of his followers in Harlem, Malcolm was slain by a burst of gunfire from the audience. Three men were later convicted of the killing, but their motive was never established, although many believed they were Black Muslim agents. *The Autobiography of Malcolm X* was published after his death.

MARSHALL, Thurgood (born 1908). Often called America's "outstanding civil-rights lawyer," Marshall is the first Negro appointed to the U.S. Supreme Court. The great-grandson of a slave and the son of a train steward, Marshall was born in Maryland. By working as a grocery clerk and waiter, he was able to support himself while a student at Lincoln University in Pennsylvania, from which he graduated in 1930. In 1933, Marshall received a law degree from Howard University. Establishing a private practice in Baltimore, he began to specialize in civil-rights cases. In 1935, Marshall won a suit against the University of Maryland Law School, forcing the school to admit a Negro student. It was the first of his many successful attacks against segregation in public education. The following year, Marshall joined the legal staff of the National Association for the Advancement of Colored People, and in 1938 he succeeded Charles H. Houston (1895–1950) as special counsel to the N.A.A.C.P. In this post for the next 25 years, Marshall fought innumerable legal battles against segregation in America. Appearing before the Supreme Court on 32 occasions, he won 29 cases. One federal circuit judge stated that "certainly no lawyer, and practically no member of the bench has Thurgood Marshall's grasp of the doctrine of law as it affects civil rights." His most outstanding victory was the 1954 Supreme Court decision holding that racial segregation in public schools was unconstitutional (*see* **Civil-rights Movement**). Marshall, who both prepared and presented the case, argued that the rule of "separate but equal" school facilities should be discarded as unconstitutional. In 1961, President **John F. Kennedy** (*see*) appointed Marshall a judge on the U.S. Court of Appeals for the Second Circuit. Four years later, President **Lyndon B. Johnson** (*see*) named him Solicitor General. Johnson appointed Marshall an Associate Justice of the Supreme Court in 1967.

MARSHALL PLAN. *See* **Truman Doctrine.**

MEANY, (William) George (born 1894). As president of the 15,000,000-member American Federation of Labor and Congress of Industrial Organization (A.F.L.-C.I.O.), Meany has concentrated on keeping peace within his mammoth organization rather than on expanding union membership or effecting social or political reforms. The son of an Irish-Catholic plumber who became president of a local union, Meany was born and raised in New York City. He became a plumber's apprentice in 1910 and a union member in 1915. In 1922, he was elected business agent for Local 463 of the plumber's union. Within 12 years, the tough spokesman for labor demands rose within union ranks to become president of the New York State Federation of Labor, a 1,000,000-member organization. He was responsible for increasing the membership despite the Depression and helped convince the state government to enact a number of prolabor laws, including an unemployment insurance act. In 1939, Meany won unanimous election as secretary-treasurer of the national American Federation of Labor (A.F.L.). In 1941, he became one of four union officials appointed by President Franklin D. Roosevelt (1882–1945) to the newly formed National Defense Mediation Board. During World War II, Meany served on the War Labor Board and fought against Con-

Thurgood Marshall and Lyndon Johnson address Negro Presidential aides.

gressional attempts to make the war effort an excuse for limiting labor's rights. On becoming president of the A.F.L. in November, 1952, Meany immediately began to seek to unite the labor movement by merging the A.F.L. with its offshoot, the C.I.O., thus healing a conflict between skilled and unskilled labor that had kept the two organizations divided since 1938. The merger was completed in December, 1955. Meany was elected president of the combined A.F.L.-C.I.O., while **Walter Reuther** (*see*), former president of the C.I.O., became a vice-president in charge of the industrial division. Since then, Meany has worked to keep his organization free of Communist and gangster influences. In December, 1957, the A.F.L.-C.I.O. expelled its largest member, the International Brotherhood of Teamsters, headed by James R. Hoffa (born 1913), after investigations led by **Robert F. Kennedy** (*see*) exposed widespread corruption in its ranks.

MUSKIE, Edmund Sixtus (born 1914). A U.S. Senator from Maine, Muskie was the Vice-Presidential candidate on the Democratic ticket headed by **Hubert H. Humphrey** (*see*) in 1968. Although the Democrats were defeated by Republicans **Richard M. Nixon** and **Spiro T. Agnew** (*see both*), Muskie gained national prominence and an enthusiastic following during the Presidential campaign. Muskie was born in Rumford, Maine, the son of a Polish immigrant (the family name was originally Marciszewski). He attended Bates College in Lewiston, Maine (1932–1936), where he majored in history, excelled as a debator, and was a member of Phi Beta Kappa, the academic honor society. After studying at Cornell University Law School

Edmund S. Muskie

(1936–1939), Muskie was admitted to the Massachusetts bar in 1939 and the Maine bar the following year. He practiced law in Waterville, Maine, until his enlistment in the naval reserve in 1942, and for the next three years he saw duty on destroyer escorts in both the Atlantic and the Pacific. Discharged as a lieutenant in 1945, Muskie returned to his law practice in Maine. The following year, running as a Democrat, he won election to the state legislature, where he served until his appointment as a district director in Maine of the Office of Price Stabilization (1951–1952). Muskie was elected governor of Maine in 1954, and he was returned to office for a second two-year term in 1956. In 1958, Muskie became the first Democrat to win popular election to the U.S. Senate from heavily Republican Maine and six years

later was reelected by a large majority. Despite an early falling-out with Senate majority leader **Lyndon B. Johnson** (*see*) after he supported liberal efforts to curb filibustering in the Senate, Muskie soon gained the respect of his colleagues for his dedication, hard work, and mastery of legislative procedures. Over the years, he compiled a progressive voting record on such issues as civil rights, antipoverty measures, aid to schools, Medicare, public-housing programs, and pollution control. He was a key sponsor of the Clear Air Act of 1963 and the Water Quality Act of 1965. In foreign affairs, Muskie has spoken in favor of international agreements to curb the spread of nuclear weapons. Early in 1968, he urged Johnson, now President, to halt the bombing of North Vietnam. Not widely known at the time of his nomination for the Vice-Presidency in August of 1968, Muskie won high praise during the ensuing campaign for his clear-headed discussion of issues and his statesmanlike conduct. He was re-elected for a third term in 1970, becoming a prime contender for his party's Presidential nomination in the 1972 elections.

N

NIXON, Richard Milhous (born 1913). When he became the 37th President of the United States, Nixon entered the White House with many years of political experience behind him, having served as both a Representative and a Senator and as Vice-President twice under **Dwight D. Eisenhower** (*see*). Born on a farm in Yorba Linda, California, of Quaker and Methodist ancestry, Nixon as a youth worked on his father's citrus farm and then in the family's combined grocery store and gasoline station in nearby Whittier, where the Nixons moved when he was nine. He graduated from Whittier College in 1934 and won a scholarship to study at Duke University Law School. After graduating in 1937, Nixon returned to Whittier, where he worked in a law firm for the next five years. Meanwhile, in 1940, he married a schoolteacher, Thelma Catherine Patricia "Pat" Ryan (born 1912). The couple later had two daughters—Patricia (born 1946) and Julie (born 1948). Nixon moved to Washington, D.C., in 1942 to work for the Office of Emergency Management. Later that year, he joined the navy as a lieutenant junior grade, serving in the South Pacific during World War II. He was a lieutenant commander when he was discharged in 1946. That same year, a California citizens' committee urged him to run for the House of Representatives on the Republican ticket against the incumbent, Horace Jerry Voorhis (born 1901), a popular Democrat who was in his fifth term. Campaigning vigorously, Nixon defeated Voorhis by 15,592 votes and was reelected in 1948. He was appointed to the select committee on foreign aid—known as the Herter Committee after its chairman, Representative Christian A. Herter (1895–1967)—that was established to study postwar economic and political problems and whose findings became the basis of the Marshall Plan (*see* **Truman Doctrine**). He served, too, on the Labor and Education Committee, where he helped draft the **Taft-Hartley Act** (*see*) of 1947. Nixon was also a member of the Committee on Un-American Activities, where he played a significant role in the investigations of Whittaker Chambers (1901–1961) and **Alger Hiss** (*see*) that led to Hiss's

conviction for perjury in 1950. Nixon thus helped to bring the "Communists in government" issue to the forefront of national politics. In 1950, he was elected to the Senate, after a bitterly fought contest in which he soundly defeated the liberal Democratic incumbent, Helen Gahagan Douglas (born 1900). As a Senator, Nixon opposed the Asian policies of President **Harry S. Truman** (*see*) and supported the plan to expand the Korean War proposed by General Douglas MacArthur (1880–1964). Nixon's youth, experience, speaking ability, and the fact that he represented the politically important state of California led to his nomination as the Vice-Presidential candidate on the Eisenhower ticket in 1952. However, soon after he was nominated, he was accused of improperly accepting $18,000 from a special fund raised by California businessmen. Nixon defended himself in a famous

nationally televised speech—known as the Checkers Speech, after his cocker spaniel, Checkers, which Nixon exhibited on television and claimed was the only personal gift he had received. The public reaction to the speech was quite favorable, and Eisenhower reconfirmed his confidence in his running mate. Following the Republican victory, Nixon became the most active Vice-President in the nation's history, partly because of the additional burdens he was forced to assume during Eisenhower's serious illnesses in 1955, 1956, and 1957, when he presided at cabinet and National Security Council meetings. He also served as chairman of groups set up to study monetary policy and to supervise the antidiscrimination clauses in contracts between the government and private concerns. He took an active role in foreign affairs, an area in which previous Vice-Presidents had

UPI

President Nixon and his family at Christmas time, 1969. From left are David and Julie Eisenhower, the President, Mrs. Nixon, and Tricia Nixon.

been relatively inactive. Nixon visited every continent except Antarctica. His two most important trips were to Latin America in May, 1958, where his car was stoned in Venezuela, and to the Soviet Union in July, 1959, where, at a trade exhibition in Moscow, he took part in a televised debate with Premier Nikita Khrushchev (born 1894). A noted anti-Communist since his Congressional days, Nixon supported Senator **Joseph R. McCarthy** (*see*) of Wisconsin in his notorious campaign to rid the State Department of alleged Communist infiltration. Among his opponents was Democratic Presidential candidate **Adlai E. Stevenson** (*see*), who described him as "the kind of politician who would cut down a redwood tree, then mount the stump and make a speech for conservation." Eisenhower, on the other hand, called him "a courageous and honest man," and the two again defeated Stevenson in the 1956 Presidential election. Nixon was the obvious choice for the Republican nomination in 1960. The ensuing campaign, in which Henry Cabot Lodge (born 1902) was his running mate, was bitter. An important feature of the 1960 race was an unprecedented series of televised debates between Nixon and the Democratic candidate, **John F. Kennedy** (*see*), whose supporters later insisted that the joint appearances were a crucial factor in Nixon's defeat. Kennedy was elected in the closest election since 1884, winning by a margin of about 100,000 votes out of the nearly 69,000,000 cast. Two years later, Nixon made an unsuccessful bid for the governorship of California but was defeated by the incumbent Democrat, Edmund G. "Pat" Brown (born 1905). That same year, he published *Six Crises,* an autobiographical account of the

major events in his political career. Nixon moved to New York City in 1963, where he practiced law and prepared himself for another—this time successful—race for the Presidency. Nixon's victorious 1968 campaign was a masterpiece of political craftsmanship. He emerged as a careful, sincere office seeker and appeared more statesmanlike and relaxed than in the past. His choice of Maryland Governor **Spiro T. Agnew** (*see*), a relatively unknown politician, as his running mate was obviously designed to win votes in the South. During the hard-fought campaign against Democrat **Hubert H. Humphrey** (*see*), Nixon pledged to end the war in Vietnam and to settle social unrest on the domestic front. Aided by a former Democrat, Strom Thurmond (born 1902) of South Carolina, Nixon defeated Humphrey by about 500,000 votes. Nixon's first 100 days in office—a traditionally crucial period—were characterized by caution. Making few new proposals and postponing most controversial decisions, Nixon concentrated on improving his public image and reorganizing the machinery of government to fit his own needs. He surprised many people by failing to deliver the annual State of the Union address to Congress in person. However, the major issue facing Nixon and the nation was the war in Vietnam. Appealing to what he called the "silent majority" of Americans, he repeatedly stated that peace was his number-one priority and began a gradual withdrawal of American forces from Vietnam, though in May, 1970, he sent U.S. troops into neighboring Cambodia in an effort to wipe out Communist-based installations there. This reawakened antiwar sentiment throughout the nation, especially in college com-

munities. In addition, Nixon alienated many Negroes by his refusal to press for public-school desegregation and his attempt to appoint a Southern conservative to the Supreme Court. Two nominees—Clement F. Haynesworth, Jr. (born 1912) of South Carolina and G. Harrold Carswell (born 1919) of Florida —were denied confirmation. A third nominee—from Minnesota —Harry A. Blackmun (born 1908) was confirmed without opposition.

NORTH ATLANTIC TREATY ORGANIZATION. Formed in 1949, The North Atlantic Treaty Organization (NATO) was the first peacetime military alliance in American history. Prompted by the Communist take-over in Czechoslovakia in February, 1948, and the Russian blockade of Berlin (*see* **Berlin Airlift**) in June of that year, President **Harry S. Truman** (*see*) determined to take steps to prevent further Soviet advances in Europe. The North Atlantic Treaty was signed in Washington on April 4, 1949, by 12 nations—Belgium, Canada, Denmark, France, Great Britain, Iceland, Italy, Luxembourg, the Netherlands, Norway, Portugal, and the United States. Each nation agreed that an armed attack against one nation would be considered an armed attack against all. The U.S. Senate approved the treaty by a vote of 82 to 13 on July 21, 1949. At subsequent conferences, with Secretary of State **Dean Acheson** (*see*) representing the United States, plans were drafted for the defense of the North Atlantic area and for the creation of a multinational military force. In October, 1949, Congress passed the Mutual Defense Assistance Act, authorizing $1,000,000,000 in military aid to NATO countries. In December, 1950, **Dwight**

D. Eisenhower (*see*) was appointed Supreme Commander of the Allied forces in Europe, with headquarters near Paris. From the start, the military branch of NATO was subject to the civilian control of the North Atlantic Council, which consists of the heads of state, foreign ministers, or ambassadors of the member nations. Greece and Turkey were admitted to NATO in 1952, and West Germany became a member in 1955. Following the announcement in 1966 by President Charles de Gaulle (born 1890) of France that nearly all French forces would be withdrawn from NATO, the civilian and military headquarters of NATO were moved to Belgium in April, 1967. Conceived as a conventional deterrent to Soviet aggression, NATO maintains 115 army divisions in Europe and a strong naval force in the North Atlantic. Some NATO units have been armed with nuclear weapons.

O

OPPENHEIMER, Julius Robert (1904–1967). A famed physicist whose work on the development of the first nuclear weapon led to his being called the father of the atomic bomb, Oppenheimer was later labeled a security risk by the Atomic Energy Commission (A.E.C.) during the "Red scare" of the 1950s because of his association with known Communists. After graduating from Harvard in 1925, Oppenheimer received his doctorate from Göttingen University in Germany. He joined the faculties of both the University of California and the California Institute of Technology in 1929 and, except for his wartime service (1943–1945), taught there until 1947. Describing his "ivory tower" years, Oppenheimer, a

scholar who could converse in eight languages, recalled, "I was almost wholly divorced from the contemporary scene in this country. I never read a newspaper or a current magazine . . . I had no radio, no telephone; I learned of the stockmarket crash . . . only long after the event; the first time I ever voted was in the Presidential election of 1936." Because of his ever-growing reputation as a scientist, Oppenheimer was put in charge of the chief laboratory of the Manhattan Project at Los Alamos, New Mexico, in the midst of World War II in March, 1943. He gathered a staff that eventually numbered 4,000 scientists and technicians to design and construct an atomic bomb. From the time the first bomb was tested in the desert on July 16, 1945, Oppenheimer seemed haunted by its implications, and he repeatedly urged international control of atomic energy. From 1947 to 1953, he was chairman of the general advisory committee to the Atomic Energy Commission. As such, he objected to the development of an even more powerful hydrogen bomb on moral grounds. However, President **Harry S. Truman** (*see*) overruled the committee and ordered work begun on the first H-bomb. Oppenheimer's associations with Communists made him a target of charges by Senator **Joseph R. McCarthy** (*see*) of Wisconsin, who was engaged in a hunt for Communists in government during the 1950s. Oppenheimer's brother and sister-in-law were both Communist Party workers, and Oppenheimer's wife had once been a member. In December, 1953, it was disclosed that President **Dwight D. Eisenhower** (*see*) had ordered Oppenheimer's security clearance suspended. A special board of the A.E.C. concluded that Oppenheimer was loyal and discreet

Oppenheimer inspects aftermath of first atomic test in 1945 with the late Maj. Gen. Leslie R. Groves.

but, by a vote of 2 to 1, it recommended the continued suspension of his top-secret clearance. He then appealed this decision to the commission itself. When the A.E.C. concurred with the board's recommendation in June, 1954, Oppenheimer returned to the Institute for Advanced Study at Princeton, New Jersey, where he had been director since 1947. He remained officially blacklisted until 1962, when President **John F. Kennedy** (*see*) invited him to the White House. In 1963, Oppenheimer received the A.E.C.'s highest award, named for the noted nuclear physicist Enrico

Fermi (1901–1954), for his outstanding contributions to nuclear physics and for laying the foundations for the peaceful uses of atomic energy. Among Dr. Oppenheimer's several books are *Science and the Common Understanding* (1954), *The Open Mind* (1955), and *Some Reflections on Science and Culture* (1960).

OSWALD, Lee Harvey. *See* **Kennedy, John F.**

P

PENTAGON PAPERS. In June, 1967, Secretary of Defense Robert S. McNamara (born 1916) commissioned an "encyclopedic and objective" study of the United States role in Indochina. The resulting top-secret work, known popularly as the Pentagon Papers, was completed in January, 1969. It covered the period from World War II to the opening of the Paris peace talks in the summer of 1968. The study filled forty-seven volumes, containing more than 4,000 pages of documents (memos, cables, orders, and proposals) and about 3,000 pages of narrative by a team of thirty-six anonymous government historians. The study came to the public's attention on June 13, 1971, when the *New York Times* began publishing a series of articles based on the papers, which had been "leaked" to it. The articles disclosed how the American government became increasingly committed to a non-Communist South Vietnam and —according to many political analysts—how a series of deceits were perpetrated on the public to support that policy. After the first three daily installments appeared, the Justice Department obtained a temporary restraining order on further publication of articles by the *Times* or by the

Washington *Post,* which had begun a similar series. The government claimed that public disclosure of the papers would cause "immediate and irreparable" harm to the nation's security. A dramatic legal battle ensued, culminating on June 30, when the Supreme Court handed down a landmark decision enabling the newspapers to continue the articles. By a vote of six to three, the Court held that freedom of the press overrode any subsidiary legal considerations. The chief source of the papers was Daniel Ellsberg (born 1931), a former Pentagon analyst and consultant to the Rand Corporation, a California-based "think tank" responsible for much of the research. He was subsequently indicted on charges of having stolen the documents.

***PUEBLO* INCIDENT.** On January 23, 1968, naval forces of Communist North Korea hijacked the *Pueblo,* a 906-ton American vessel that had been converted from a freighter into a highly sophisticated electronic reconnaisance ship for surveillance missions. The North Korean government claimed that the ship was within the 12-mile limit that it claims as its territorial waters and that the *Pueblo* "was carrying out hostile activities." The *Pueblo* was manned by a crew of 83, which included its skipper, Commander Lloyd M. Bucher (born 1927), five other officers, and two civilian map specialists. Her mission was to gather intelligence in the Sea of Japan, and she sailed off the coast of North Korea and close to the ports of Wonsan, North Korea, where Russia maintains a fighter-plane base, and Vladivostok, the Russian Pacific fleet headquarters. At about noon on January 23, a North Korean torpedo boat ordered the *Pueblo,* then in the second week of a

planned four-week tour, to heave to, threatening to fire if disobeyed. Commander Bucher maintained his ship's course but reduced her speed. An hour later, two more North Korean torpedo boats and a submarine chaser surrounded the *Pueblo,* while two jet fighters circled overhead. Bucher first considered these maneuvers as merely attempts at harassment. However, suddenly he radioed navy headquarters in Yokosuka, Japan, "These guys are serious." The North Koreans had opened fire prior to boarding the *Pueblo.* The crew tried to destroy classified documents and electronic gear worth millions of dollars by fire or with axes, sledgehammers, and hand grenades. Several men were seriously injured in the attempt. One, Duane Hodges, later died of his wounds. At 1:45 P.M. the North Koreans swarmed aboard and "requested" that the *Pueblo* head for Wonsan, about two hours away. Bucher reported he was "going off the air" at 2:32 P.M., when the North Koreans decided to tow the ship into port. As soon as the boarding of the *Pueblo* became certain, Bucher's reports had been relayed through Yokosuka to the office of the navy commander in chief of the Pacific fleet in Honolulu and to Washington, D.C. However, no navy or airforce planes had been immediately available for a rescue mission. Secretary of Defense Robert S. McNamara (born 1916) was alerted shortly after the incident occurred, about 15 minutes before Bucher radioed his final message. President **Lyndon B. Johnson** *(see),* who was not informed until the *Pueblo* had almost reached Wonsan, activated 28 air reserve units of the national guard, air force, and navy, adding a total force of 14,787 civilians to U.S. forces and ordered nearly

300 late-model planes to South Korean bases. The 75,700-ton nuclear carrier *Enterprise* and its task force was ordered to stand by off the North Korean coast. The President acted with caution, despite the desire of the American public for immediate and forceful retaliation. Secretary of State **Dean Rusk** (*see*) described the incident as "an act of war." A planning committee, which the President had formed, decided to take the matter to the United Nations. It was felt that the United States, already deeply involved in the Vietnam war, could ill afford a confrontation also with the North Koreans. Johnson went on national television on January 26 to pledge that "we shall continue to use every means available to find a prompt and peaceful solution." That same day, at the U.N., Ambassador **Arthur Goldberg** (*see*) called on the Security Council to "act with the greatest urgency." However, the North Korean government declared that it would not be bound by any U.N. resolutions. Meanwhile, numerous reports of the *Pueblo* crew's alleged confessions to acts of espionage, aggression, and violation of international law were released by the North Koreans. As the months passed, American representatives met repeatedly with those of North Korea to obtain the crew's release. On September 30, 1968, eight months after the capture of the *Pueblo*, the North Koreans agreed to free her crew if the United States signed a document that would admit the *Pueblo's* guilt in intruding in North Korea's territorial waters, apologize for acts of espionage, and admit that the confessions of the crew were in fact true. On December 17, 1968, in Panmunjom, South Korea, during the 26th meeting between the United States and North Korea

on the *Pueblo,* U.S. Army General Gilbert H. Woodward, top U.N. member of the armistice commission, signed the document. At the same time he denounced it, saying, "The position of the U.S. has been that the ship was not engaged in illegal activities . . . I will sign the document to free the crew and only to free the crew." On Christmas Eve, 1968, the 82 surviving crew members and the body of Duane Hodges arrived back in the United States. Bucher and his men had suffered 11 months of brutality in a North Korean prison camp. They had been repeatedly beaten and tortured in efforts to force confessions from them. At the hearings of a naval court of inquiry at Coronado, California, in February, 1969, the navy disclosed that shortly after the *Pueblo's* capture two destroyers under heavy air cover had been ordered to sail for Wonsan to escort the *Pueblo* to safety. However, the plan had been vetoed by the President to avoid hostilities and to prevent the certain death of the *Pueblo's* crew. The hearing corroborated Bucher's testimony that the ship could not have been defended, and that he had pointed out its lack of armament while the vessel was being refitted for its surveillance mission. The *Pueblo* had gone to sea manned by only three 3.50-caliber machine guns, while North Korean vessels carried 25-millimeter anti-aircraft guns. Lieutenant Stephen R. Harris (born 1930), the ship's security officer, was severely criticized for his failure to destroy 2,000 pounds of classified documents, although equipment to quickly destroy such a vast quantity of paper was not available. Ultimately, Secretary of the Navy John Chafee (born 1922), together with other members of the navy's top command,

Samuel T. Rayburn

agreed that the responsibility for the *Pueblo's* capture had to be shared by all levels of command. It was indicated that the *Pueblo,* which has not yet been returned to the United States, had not been supported by the air cover normally supplied ships on dangerous spy missions.

R

RAYBURN, Samuel Taliferro (1882–1961). Aptly known as Mr. Speaker, Rayburn fulfilled a boyhood ambition to be Speaker of the House of Representatives, serving in that post more than twice as long as any other Congressman. He was also an influential Democrat during his 48 years of continual service in the House. "Mr. Sam," as he was also called, was born in Tennessee and grew up in northeast Texas, where he helped on his father's 40-acre cotton farm. When he was 18, he entered East Texas Normal School (now East Texas State University) and worked at odd jobs and as a teacher to earn his Bachelor of Science degree. After working two more years as a country schoolteacher, Rayburn was elected to the Texas legislature in 1906. It was the first of 28 consecutive election campaigns he waged without defeat. He served three terms in the legislature (1907–1912), the last term as the 29-year-old speaker of the Texas House of Representatives. Meanwhile, he studied law at the University of Texas and was admitted to the bar. At 30, Rayburn was elected to the first of his 25 terms (1913–1961) in the U.S. House of Representatives and soon attracted the attention and earned the respect of President Woodrow Wilson (1856–1924). Later, as chairman of the Interstate and Foreign Commerce Committee from 1931 to 1937, he sponsored many of the New Deal measures of President Franklin D. Roosevelt (1882–1945). He became Speaker on September 16, 1940. Except for four years when the Republicans controlled Congress (1947–1949 and 1953–1955), Rayburn held the post until his death. On January 30, 1951, he broke the previous longevity record of Henry Clay (1777–1852), who had held the office of Speaker for eight years, four months, and 11 days. As Speaker during the administration of **Harry S. Truman** (*see*), Rayburn opposed Truman's efforts to regulate natural-gas and oil producers. However, he backed Truman's foreign-aid and trade policies, including the Marshall Plan (*see* **Truman Doctrine**). Together with his protégé, Senate majority leader **Lyndon B. Johnson** (*see*) of Texas, Rayburn effectively worked with President **Dwight D. Eisenhower** (*see*) in formulating a modified version of a civil-rights program that he had opposed in the past. This led, in 1957, to the enactment of

the first major civil-rights act since the Reconstruction era and, three years later, to a second civil-rights measure—both designed chiefly to protect the voting rights of Southern Negroes. Rayburn's control in the House was based on his ability to conciliate and, like Johnson, compromise. "You cannot lead people by trying to drive them," he said. "Persuasion and reason are the only ways to lead them. In that way the Speaker has influence and power in the House." A familiar figure as the gavel-wielding chairman at the Democratic National Conventions in 1948, 1952, and 1956, the bald, stocky Rayburn declined that role in 1960 to back Johnson for the Presidency. However, when **John F. Kennedy** (*see*) won the nomination and then the election, Rayburn tried to work with Kennedy in overcoming conservative opposition to the new President's legislative program. "I always say without prefix, without suffix and without apology," he declared, "that I am a Democrat." Rayburn was able to get the influential House Rules Committee enlarged so that liberal members could bring to a vote Kennedy's proposals, and he was successful in winning early support for liberal housing, minimum-wage, and urban-renewal programs. Not so successful were his efforts regarding a broad federal aid-to-education bill and other Kennedy-sponsored measures. .

REUTHER, Walter Philip (1907–1970). One of the founders of the Congress of Industrial Organizations (C.I.O.) in the 1930s, Reuther successfully opposed Communist infiltration in the 1940s and was the C.I.O.'s president when it merged with the American Federation of Labor (A.F.L.) led by **George Meany** (*see*) in 1955. Well-educated, articulate, and scrupu-

lously honest, Reuther, the son of a German-born labor organizer, was born in Wheeling, West Virginia. Although he left school to go to work at the age of 15, he subsequently completed high school and later attended Wayne State University in Detroit in his spare time. At 16, he led his first protest. It was against the Wheeling Steel Corporation, whose seven-day work week prevented him from taking part in his family's Sunday-afternoon discussions of current issues. The protest cost him his 40¢-an-hour job. Two years later, Reuther went to Detroit, where he became a shop foreman in a Ford Motor Company plant. Discharged by Ford in 1932 for his union activities, Reuther went to England, where he worked briefly in mines and factories and then spent more than a year in a Ford-built automotive plant in Russia. Both the working conditions in Russia and the Communist system appalled him. After visiting India and Japan, Reuther returned to Detroit and became active in the early organizing of the United Automobile Workers of America (U.A.W.). He led one of the first U.A.W. sit-down strikes in 1936. At the same time, he helped organize the C.I.O. An offshoot of the older A.F.L., the C.I.O. formally broke away from the parent union in 1938. The breakaway was led by John L. Lewis (1880–1968) and other union leaders, Reuther among them, who believed that the A.F.L., traditionally a craft union, had been too slow in organizing unskilled production-line workers. After he became vice-president of the U.A.W. in 1942, Reuther advocated active support of World War II and devised the plan that converted automobile factories to the manufacture of airplanes. After the war, he was elected president of the U.A.W. and a vice-president of the C.I.O. He subsequently led successful strikes to gain cost-of-living increases, pension plans, and other fringe benefits for workers, while at the same time leading a bitter struggle to rid the C.I.O. of Communists. Denouncing the Communists as "colonial agents using the trade union movement as a basis of operation in order to carry out the needs of the Soviet Foreign Office," he declared that they had no right "to peddle the Communist Party line with a C.I.O. label on the wrapper." In April, 1948, a shotgun blast from an unidentified assailant severely wounded Reuther, and an unsuccessful attempt to dynamite the U.A.W. offices was made in December, 1949. In 1951, most Communist unions had finally been driven out of the C.I.O. By then, the A.F.L. and C.I.O. had been brought closer together by the C.I.O.'s troubles with Communists and the A.F.L.'s similar problems in ridding itself of hoodlums. In addition, both unions were now trying to recruit members from some of the same industries. In November, 1952, when the presidents of both federations—Philip Murray (1886–1952) of the C.I.O. and William Green (1873–1952) of the A.F.L., who had been rivals for many years—died, a merger became imminent. The new heads of the unions, Reuther of the C.I.O. and Meany of the A.F.L., began in April, 1953, to work out a series of agreements that resulted in a formal merger in December, 1955. Meany was elected president of the combined A.F.L.-C.I.O., while Reuther became vice-president in charge of the industrial division. In December, 1966, Reuther's U.A.W. charged that the A.F.L.-C.I.O. was failing to fulfill the merger aims. Three months later, he resigned from the executive council of the A.F.L.-C.I.O. because he disagreed with the

council's support of the Vietnam War and domestic policies of President **Lyndon B. Johnson** (*see*). He later threatened to withdraw the U.A.W. from the A.F.L.-C.I.O. on the same issues but did not do so. The recipient of numerous awards and honorary degrees, Reuther was named in 1968 the "greatest living U.S. labor leader" by 48 newspaper editors. He and his wife were killed in a plane crash in northern Michigan.

RICKOVER, Hyman George (born 1900). A pioneer in the development of atomic sea power, Rickover is known as the father of the nuclear submarine. As a child, he came to America from Russia with his family in 1905. After graduating from Annapolis in 1922, he served five years' duty at sea before returning there to study electrical engineering. In 1929, he earned a master's degree from Columbia University. The following year, Rickover received submarine training at New London, Connecticut. In 1939, he was assigned to the Bureau of Ships in Washington, D.C., and during World War II served as head of its electrical section. At the end of the war, Rickover was assigned to the Atomic Energy Commission's Manhattan Project at Oak Ridge, Tennessee, which took part in the developing of the atomic bomb. As assistant director of operations, he planned the construction of the first nuclear-powered submarine, the *Nautilus,* which was launched in 1954. To facilitate cooperation between the A.E.C. and the navy, Rickover was made chief of the Naval Reactors Branch of the A.E.C. and head of the Nuclear Propulsion Division of the navy's Bureau of Ships. His civilian post, however, brought the outspoken naval officer into conflict with his superiors. When the

navy did not promote Captain Rickover to an admiral's rank in 1951 and 1952, he faced compulsory retirement, until Congress pressured the navy into making him a rear admiral in 1953. When a similar situation arose five years later, Congressional pressure again forced his promotion to vice admiral. Three years later, President **John F. Kennedy** (*see*) ordered the navy to keep Rickover beyond the official retirement age. That same year, he received the Distinguished Service Medal for his "skillful technical direction, unusual foresight, and unswerving perseverance" in the field of naval nuclear propulsion. Rickover, who established naval training schools at New London, Connecticut, in 1956 and at Mare Island, California, in 1958, has also been interested in civilian education. He published two books on the subject, *Education and Freedom* (1959) and *Swiss Schools and Ours: Why Theirs Are Better* (1962). Although his name was finally put on the navy's retired list in 1964, Rickover remains active as Deputy Commander for Nuclear Propulsion, Naval Ship Systems Command.

ROBINSON, Jack Roosevelt ("Jackie") (born 1919). For nine

Jackie Robinson

years a member of the Brooklyn Dodgers, Robinson was the first Negro to play major-league baseball. The Georgia-born athlete was raised in Pasadena, California, where he excelled in high-school sports. Later, as a student at the University of California from 1939 to 1941, he starred in basketball, football, baseball, and track. During World War II, Robinson served as a second lieutenant in the 27th Cavalry. After the war, he played shortstop for the Kansas City Monarchs, a team in the Negro American Baseball League. His high batting average attracted the attention of Branch Rickey (1881–1965), president of the Brooklyn Dodgers, who in 1945 signed him to play with the Montreal Royals, a Dodger farm club in the International League. During his first season, Robinson played second base, stole 40 bases, and batted .349, an average that earned him the league championship. The following year, he moved up to the Brooklyn Dodgers, becoming the first Negro to play in major-league competition. At the end of the season, the versatile second baseman received the National League's Rookie of the Year Award. In 1949, he was named the league's Most Valuable Player. The same year his .342 average earned him the league's batting crown. When he retired in 1956 after 10 seasons with the Dodgers, Robinson had compiled an overall batting average of .311. Six years later, he was elected to the National Baseball Hall of Fame, the first Negro so honored. Robinson became a vice-president of a chain of coffee shops. He also contributed a sports column to the New York *Post* in 1959. In 1964, he left his job to be a deputy director of the unsuccessful campaign of Governor Nelson Rockefeller (born 1908)

of New York for the Republican Presidential nomination. He later served as the governor's special assistant for community affairs and became chairman of the board of the Freedom National Bank in New York City.

ROSENBERG SPY CASE. On June 19, 1953, Julius Rosenberg (1918–1953) and his wife, Ethel (1921–1953), were electrocuted for treason in New York's Sing Sing Prison as a result of one of the most spectacular spy cases in American history. Beginning in

glass stole data that included sketches of the detonating device and other parts of the atom bomb that was dropped on Nagasaki, Japan, in August, 1945. Earlier, in February of that year, Rosenberg was suspended from the army on the recommendation of his commanding officer, who had been informed that Rosenberg was a member of the Communist Party. In 1950, both Rosenbergs were arrested by agents of the Federal Bureau of Investigation (*see* **Hoover, J. Edgar**) and charged with con-

Spies Julius and Ethel Rosenberg posed a few days before their execution.

1940, Rosenberg, then an engineer with the U.S. Army Signal Corps, and his wife started selling American military information to Russian agents. In 1944–45, they turned over vital information concerning the atomic bomb. They obtained this material from Mrs. Rosenberg's brother, David Greenglass (born 1922), an army sergeant who at that time was the foreman of an atomic assembly plant at Los Alamos, New Mexico. Green-

spiracy to disclose atomic and other secrets to the Soviet Union during World War II. Their widely publicized trial opened on March 6, 1951. On April 5, they were found guilty of treason under the Espionage Act of 1917, which makes the death sentence mandatory. Greenglass, who was the government's chief witness, supplied most of the evidence against them. He testified that the Rosenbergs had turned over nuclear plans to Harry Gold (born 1910), a Philadelphia chemist, who was the contact man and courier between the couple and Russian agents. Among those agents was Anatoli Yakovlev, who in the 1940s was the Russian vice-consul in New York City. Yakovlev, who was indicted in absentia at the same time as the Rosenbergs, had fled to Russia in December, 1946. Gold received a 30-year prison sentence in December, 1950, for his part in the conspiracy. Gold also had connections with two other Russian agents, Alan Nunn May (born 1911), a British scientist, and Dr. Klaus Fuchs (born 1911), a German-born British subject who was an atomic physicist. Fuchs had been involved in the development of the atomic bomb at Los Alamos in 1945. Both May and Fuchs were given prison sentences in Great Britain. Another member of the spy ring, Morton Sobell (born 1917), an electronics engineer, was also convicted with the Rosenbergs and was sentenced to 30 years in prison. The trial provoked worldwide interest, and many non-Communists, including religious leaders of various faiths, believed that the Rosenbergs' sentence of death was too severe and urged clemency. Numerous appeals for a rehearing were made, and several stays of execution were granted the couple. The Rosenbergs made two appeals for clemency to President **Dwight D. Eisenhower** (*see*), the last one on the day before their execution, but all attempts to save them failed. The Rosenbergs were the first American civilians executed for treason. After his release by the British in 1953, May went to Ghana to teach, while Fuchs, who was freed in 1959, settled in East Germany. Gold was released on parole in 1965, and Sobell was freed four years later. Green-

glass, who had received only a 15-year sentence because he had cooperated with federal authorities, was released in 1960 after serving nine and a half years.

RUBY, Jack. *See* **Kennedy, John F.**

RUSK, (David) Dean (born 1909). As Secretary of State under Presidents **John F. Kennedy** and **Lyndon B. Johnson** (*see both*), Rusk became identified as one of the leading proponents of American policy in Vietnam. Born in Georgia, Rusk attended North Carolina's Davidson College from 1927 to 1931, won a Rhodes Scholarship, and did graduate work at Oxford University, England, taking a master's degree in 1934. He then taught at Mills College in California, becoming dean of the faculty in 1938. At the same time, he completed his legal training at the University of California. Early in World War II, Rusk was assigned to army intelligence. He participated in two campaigns in Burma and became deputy chief of staff to General Joseph Stilwell (1883–1946). After the war, Rusk joined the State Department. After serving briefly as a delegate to the United Nations, he was the first appointee to the newly created post of Assistant Secretary of State for United Nations affairs in 1949. As Assistant Secretary of State for Far Eastern affairs in 1950, Rusk played a major role in deliberations leading to the United States' involvement in the Korean War. He believed that intervention would prevent further Communist aggression in the Far East. During the conflict, he supported President **Harry S. Truman** (*see*) in recalling General Douglas MacArthur (1880–1964), who wanted to attack China. In 1951, Rusk assisted Secretary of State **John**

WIDE WORLD

Dean Rusk

Foster Dulles (*see*) in negotiating a peace treaty with Japan. He left the State Department in 1952 to become president of the Rockefeller Foundation. For nearly nine years he directed the distribution of funds—about $250,000,000 in all—for various projects, including aid to other nations. He resigned in 1960, when President-elect Kennedy named him Secretary of State. Under Kennedy, Rusk had little opportunity to initiate foreign policy, and he acted mainly on directives from the President. Rusk did stress a need for the "quiet diplomacy" of trained specialists, rather than well-publicized summit meetings between heads of state. He emphasized the importance of aiding underdeveloped nations and backed Kennedy's aim to negotiate with the Communists from a position of strength. In his first few months in office, Rusk was confronted with a series of world crises, including the threat of a Communist take-over in Laos (he helped negotiate a cease-fire there in May, 1961), and the ill-fated **Bay of Pigs invasion** (*see*) in Cuba. After Kennedy's assassination in 1963, President Johnson asked him to stay in his post. With Congressional approval of the **Gulf of Tonkin Resolution** (*see*) in 1964, a massive buildup of American military forces occurred in Vietnam. "We are there," Rusk told the Senate Armed Services Subcommittee in 1966, "to see to it that North Vietnam does not seize South Vietnam by force, and we will accomplish that result." He denied the existence of much ground fighting, although more than 350,000 American soldiers were stationed there. The next year, Senator Strom Thurmond (born 1902) of South Carolina accused Rusk of inadequate efforts to win the war. The secretary's response was that the use of nuclear weapons was unjustifiable. "We have to try to find a reasonable and rational way to do what is required to stop aggression," he declared. Rusk left office in January, 1969, and a year later accepted a teaching position at the University of Georgia.

S

SANDBURG, Carl (1878–1967). One of America's most famous and best-loved poets, Sandburg was also a folk singer and the author of a definitive six-volume biography of Abraham Lincoln (1809–1865). The first two volumes of his masterpiece are entitled *Abraham Lincoln: The Prairie Years* (1926), and the final four volumes are *Abraham Lincoln: The War Years* (1939). This work, which required years of research, depicts Lincoln as the embodiment of the American democratic spirit. It won Sandburg the Pulitzer Prize for history in 1940. Born in Galesburg, Illinois, Sandburg attended public schools until he was 13. He then worked at various trades in the Middle West and served in Puerto Rico during the Spanish-American War. He attended

WIDE WORLD

Carl Sandburg

(1898–1902) Lombard College (now Knox College) in Galesburg but never graduated, and he later worked as a newspaperman in Milwaukee, Wisconsin, and as secretary from 1910 to 1912 to that city's Socialist mayor, Emil Seidel (1864–1947). Sandburg later moved to Chicago, where he continued his journalistic career and enjoyed his first poetic success when several of his poems appeared in *Poetry* magazine in 1914. Among these poems was "Chicago," in which he caught the throbbing energy of that metropolis, describing it as

Hog Butcher for the World,
Tool Maker, Stacker of Wheat,
Player with Railroads and the
Nation's Freight Handler;
Stormy, husky, brawling,
City of the Big Shoulders.

"Chicago" was also the title piece of his volume *Chicago Poems* (1916), which included "Fog," a poem whose famous opening line is, "*The fog comes on little cat feet.*" This volume, together with *Cornhuskers* (1918, winner of a special Pulitzer award in 1919), *Smoke and Steel* (1920), and *Slabs of the Sunburnt West* (1922), established Sandburg's reputation as one of the nation's most original and vital poets. His free-form verses captured the American idiom—especially the rugged Middle Western speech—and contained many lyrical passages. During the 1920s and '30s, Sandburg traveled all over the country, reading his poetry and singing folk songs, accompanying himself on the guitar. He published two collections of local ballads, *The American Songbag* (1927) and *The New American Songbag* (1950). Sandburg's later volumes of poetry included *Good Morning, America* (1928), *The People, Yes* (1936), *Complete Poems* (1950, winner of the Pulitzer Prize for poetry in 1951), *Harvest Poems, 1910–1960* (1960), and *Honey and Salt* (1963). He also wrote several children's books, such as *Rootabaga Stories* (1922); some prose works, including *Steichen the Photographer* (1929), a biography of his brother-in-law Edward Steichen (born 1879); *Remembrance Rock* (1948), a novel; and *Always the Young Strangers* (1953), which is about his youth and from which he excerpted *Prairie Town Boy* (1955) for children.

SIRHAN, Sirhan. *See* **Kennedy, Robert F.**

SOUTHEAST ASIA TREATY ORGANIZATION. Primarily designed to block Communist expansion in Asia, SEATO was created in 1954 by the United States, Great Britain, France, Australia, New Zealand, Pakistan, Thailand, and the Philippines. The SEATO provisions were agreed upon in June of that year at a meeting in Washington, D.C., between President **Dwight D. Eisenhower,** his Secretary of State, **John Foster Dulles** (*see both*), British Prime Minister Winston Churchill (1874–1965), and Churchill's foreign secretary, Anthony Eden (born 1897). On September 8, 1954, at Manila, the eight member nations signed the Southeast Asia Collective Defense Treaty, which became effective on February 19, 1955. The treaty area covers the general area of Southeast Asia, including the territories of its members, and the general area of the southwest Pacific. It specifically excludes, however, both Formosa (Taiwan), where the Nationalist Chinese government is based, and the British colony of Hong Kong. The Republic of Vietnam and the kingdoms of Cambodia and Laos—all of which were part of French Indochina before 1954—were accorded military protection under the treaty, although they are not members. A defensive alignment, SEATO, unlike the **North Atlantic Treaty Organization** (*see*), has no military units directly attached to it. However, military cooperation has included joint maneuvers, arrangements to coordinate military forces, and the strengthening of the armed forces of the Asian members. Collective security is guaranteed under the treaty in the case of armed attack in the area against any of the member nations, or against any other government in the area that requests and is unanimously granted aid. The United States added a proviso to the treaty that says it is only bound to act in the case of Communist aggression but will consider its response "in the event of other aggression or armed attack." Similarly, the four SEATO members belonging to the British Commonwealth of Nations—Australia, New Zealand, Pakistan, and Britain herself—indicated that they would take exception against possible action against any other Commonwealth member, such as India. Although SEATO was

formed following Communist China's threats to peace after the Korean War and France's withdrawal from Indochina, many nations in the treaty area refused to participate in any accord. India, Indonesia, Burma, and Malaya have criticized the organization because it is dominated by Western powers. Following the reported North Vietnamese attack on two American warships in August, 1964, Congress approved the **Gulf of Tonkin Resolution** giving President **Lyndon B. Johnson** (*see both*) the authority "to take all necessary steps" to help any nation covered by the SEATO treaty "requesting assistance in defense of its freedom." Although Thai, Filipino, Australian, and New Zealand forces were sent to Vietnam, the United States never invoked the mutual-aid provision of the SEATO treaty, because Britain and France both declined to support collective action. France and Pakistan have since withdrawn all military ties with SEATO.

STEVENSON, Adlai Ewing (1900–1965). Twice the unsuccessful Democratic Presidential candidate in the 1950s, Stevenson became a leading world statesman and the chief spokesman for the United States in the United Nations. The grandson and namesake of Vice-President Adlai E. Stevenson (1835–1914), Stevenson was born in California, where his father was an executive for the newspaper and mining interests of William Randolph Hearst (1863–1951). He was raised in his parents' hometown of Bloomington, Illinois, where the family moved when Adlai was six. After graduating from Princeton in 1922 and from Northwestern University Law School, he was admitted to the Illinois bar in 1926 and joined a Chicago law firm in

1927. Four years later, he went to Washington as special counsel for the Agricultural Adjustment Administration and then the Federal Alcohol Control Administration. Returning to Chicago in 1934, he continued to practice law and joined the Chicago Council on Foreign Relations. In the late 1930s, as war broke out in Europe, Stevenson spoke out against isolationism in his native state. From July, 1941, to April, 1944, he served as a special assistant to the Secretary of the Navy. In 1943, he led a mission to plan the rehabilitation of Italy and the following year to survey the U.S. Army Air Force in Britain and on the continent. In February, 1945, Stevenson returned to Washington as an assistant to the Secretary of State, Edward R. Stettinius, Jr. (1900–1949), and helped to plan the charter meeting of the United Nations in San Francisco. Late in 1945, he went to London as the secretary's deputy and as chief of the U.S. delegation at the U.N. preparatory commission. In early 1946, he was senior adviser to the American delegation at the first General Assembly sessions in London. He was a delegate at the second and third sessions in New York in 1946 and 1947. Although he had never before run for public office, Stevenson decided to seek the governorship of Illinois in 1948 and won with a plurality of 572,067 votes. As governor, he was responsible for a number of major reforms. He changed the basis of the state-police force from political appointment to the merit system and then used the cleaned-up force to smash gambling interests. He reorganized state mental hospitals, doubled state aid to schools, modernized the highway system, and abolished nearly 1,300 unnecessary state jobs. By January, 1952, Stevenson had become a prominent figure in Democratic circles. Speculation ran high that he would run for President despite his own avowal that he planned to run for a second term as governor. In July, at the Democratic National Convention, Stevenson was drafted on the third ballot. As a campaigner, Stevenson, an articulate and urbane intellectual, lost large blocks of votes because of his uncompromising candor. In addition, he was identified with the Democratic administration, in power for the past 20 years, and was pitted against **Dwight D. Eisenhower** (*see*), a war hero whose national popularity had prompted both the Democratic and Republican parties to seek him as a candidate. Stevenson polled about 27,000,000 popular votes against Eisenhower's almost 34,000,000 and won only 89 electoral votes to Eisenhower's 442. Stevenson's concession speech closed with a touch of the wry humor that had become his trademark: "Someone asked me, as I came down the street, how I felt, and I was reminded of a story that a fellow townsman of ours used to tell—Abraham Lincoln. They asked him how he felt once after an unsuccessful election. He said he felt like a little boy who had stubbed his toe in the dark. He said that he was too old to cry, but it hurt too much to laugh." With the election over, Stevenson continued to head the Democratic Party, taking a five-month world tour and campaigning actively in the Congressional elections of 1954, an overall Democratic victory. During this campaign, Stevenson charged that the Republican Party was "half McCarthy and half Eisenhower." The reference to **Joseph R. McCarthy** (*see*) of Wisconsin was an attack on that Senator's notorious witch-hunt. Eisenhower's

Vice-President, **Richard M. Nixon** (*see*), countered by accusing Stevenson of unconsciously spreading Communist propaganda. In 1956, Stevenson was renominated by the Democrats for President, beating out Estes Kefauver (1903–1963) of Tennessee and New York Governor Averell Harriman (born 1891). Eisenhower ridiculed Stevenson's request for an end to aboveground nuclear testing as a "moratorium on common sense," although two years after his reelection the former general made the same request. Stevenson was again defeated—this time polling only 73 electoral votes to Eisenhower's 457. From 1955 through 1960, Stevenson was a partner of law firms in Chicago and New York. He became a belated candidate in the 1960 Democratic convention but lost out to **John F. Kennedy** (*see*). In December, 1960, President-elect Kennedy appointed Stevenson ambassador to the United Nations. Once an advocate of admitting Communist China to the U.N., he reversed his stand to conform with Kennedy's foreign policy. Stevenson sometimes chafed at his job, telling a reporter, "There is a disadvantage in being anywhere other than the seat of power. And every issue that comes to the U.N. has its antecedents before it gets here." However, his logic and language were assets in U.N. debates. The **Bay of Pigs invasion** (*see*) in 1961 was the cause of embarrassment to Stevenson, who had not been adequately briefed by the President about the United States' involvement. He also had to defend the American position in the Cuban missile crisis with Russia in October, 1962. After Kennedy's assassination, President **Lyndon B. Johnson** (*see*) reconfirmed Stevenson's appointment. In June, 1965, in a

speech at Harvard University, Stevenson summed up his view of current foreign policy: "If total isolationism is no answer, total intervention is no answer, either. . . . In this twilight of power, there is no quick path to a convenient light switch." The next month, he confided to friends his intention to resign soon. A few days later, he suffered a heart attack on a London street and died.

T

TAFT, Robert Alphonso (1889–1953). "Mr. Republican"—as this Ohio Senator was called—was known for his conservatism, isolationist principles, and personal integrity. The eldest son of the 27th President of the United States, William Howard Taft (1857–1930), he tried three times to win his party's nomination for the Presidency, coming closest in 1952 when he lost to General **Dwight D. Eisenhower** (*see*). Taft was born in Cincinnati and graduated from Yale in 1910. Three years later, he earned his law degree at Harvard. He subsequently practiced in Cincinnati and, during World War I, served as counsel for the U.S. Food Administration and the American Relief Administration in Europe. In 1921, Taft was elected to the Ohio legislature (1921–1926 and 1931–1932). He was elected to the first of three terms (1939–1953) in the U.S. Senate in 1938. In Congress, Taft soon achieved eminence for his opposition to the New Deal programs of President Franklin D. Roosevelt (1882–1945). Taft also led the isolationist faction in Congress, believing, after Germany began World War II in Europe, that a negotiated peace with the Nazi government was still possible. However, after the Japanese attacked Pearl Harbor on December 7, 1941, he backed America's war effort and proposed that a permanent peacemaking organization be established at war's end. Taft reverted to his isolationist views in his

Robert A. Taft

1948 Presidential campaign, opposing both the Marshall Plan (*see* **Truman Doctrine**) and the **North Atlantic Treaty Organization** (*see*). He said the United States should abandon world leadership, "living so well at home that all other nations would wonder, envy, and decide to emulate us." At the same time, he thought that the authority of the United Nations should be strengthened. The most controversial accomplishment of Taft's Senate career was his drafting and co-sponsoring, with Representative Fred A. Hartley, Jr. (1902–1969) of New Jersey, of the Labor-Management Relations Act, which became known as the **Taft-Hartley Act** (*see*). Passed by Congress on June 23, 1947, over the veto of President **Harry S. Truman** (*see*), the act was designed to curtail the powers of labor unions and make them subject to government control. Its provisions had the effect of alienating organized labor by, among other things, requiring union leaders to take

loyalty oaths and empowering the federal government to obtain an 80-day injunction against any strike that endangers the "national health or safety." (Although later modified, the essential provisions of the act still remain in effect and have been employed to block a number of crippling nationwide work stoppages.) After failing to become the Republican Presidential candidate in both 1940 and 1948, Taft made a final attempt in 1952. Although he was initially the front-runner in the contest against Eisenhower and had the backing of party professionals, the drive to nominate the General, a national hero, gained momentum and delegate strength. At the party's convention in Chicago that summer, the Eisenhower forces succeeded in changing a convention rule, on the seating of contested delegates, to their benefit. As a result, Eisenhower was able to win 595 votes to Taft's 500 on the first ballot and, when Minnesota switched its votes, clinched the nomination. That autumn, Eisenhower and Taft had a public reconciliation. Taft subsequently became a trusted adviser to Eisenhower, who was elected President over Democrat **Adlai E. Stevenson** (*see*). Taft also exerted a wide influence as Senate majority leader. However, in June, 1953, he disclosed that he had a serious illness and resigned from the Senate leadership. He died soon afterward of cancer. A 100-foot-tall Taft Memorial Bell Tower, situated near the Capitol, was dedicated in his honor in 1959.

TAFT-HARTLEY ACT. Enacted in June, 1947, over the veto of President **Harry S. Truman** (*see*) and despite the opposition of organized labor, the Taft-Hartley Act placed limitations on the conduct of unions in labor-

management disputes. The provisions of the bill, officially known as the Labor-Management Relations Act, amended the National Labor Relations Act (Wagner Act) of 1935 that had placed restrictions on management. The Taft-Hartley Act authorized the federal government to issue an 80-day injunction against any strike that would endanger the "national health or safety." It also prohibited direct union contributions to political campaigns, and required the public disclosure of a union's financial records. In addition, the act banned the closed shop, permitted employers to sue unions for broken contracts or unfair labor practices, required unions to give 60 days' notice of their intent to strike, and required union leaders to file affidavits that they were not Communists. An especially controversial provision, Section 14-b, permitted states to enact so-called right-to-work laws that made it possible for a worker to hold a job without being required to join a union. The sponsors of the measure were two Republicans, Senator **Robert A. Taft** (*see*) of Ohio and Representative Fred A. Hartley, Jr. (1902–1969) of New Jersey. Republican victories in the Congressional elections of 1946 enabled the House to override Truman's veto by a vote of 331 to 83. The Senate overrode the President's veto by a vote of 68 to 25. Soon after its passage, union leaders condemned the act as a "slave bill" and campaigned for its repeal. Organized labor supported Truman in 1948 after he came out strongly in favor of repeal, but he was unable to win Congressional approval of repeal. The Landrum-Griffin Bill of 1959, which dealt primarily with the relationship of individual union members to a union, repealed the section of the Taft-Hartley Act requiring a loyalty oath from union leaders. In 1965, President **Lyndon B. Johnson** (*see*) urged repeal of Section 14-b. A bill was passed in the House of Representatives, but a filibuster in the Senate, led by Republican Senator **Everett M. Dirksen** (*see*) of Illinois prevented its passage. Right-to-work laws are still in effect in many states.

TRUMAN, Harry S. (*Continued from Volume 15*). With the end of World War II, the man thrust into the Presidency by the death of Franklin D. Roosevelt (1882–1945) faced complex domestic problems and steadily increasing tensions between the United States and Russia. On August 18, 1945—four days after Japan's surrender—Truman issued a "hold-the-line order" that extended wartime controls on production, wages, and prices. Less than a month later, he recommended to a joint session of Congress federal aid to education, an increase in the minimum wage, a medical-insurance plan, and civil-rights legislation. The speech set the basic outline of Truman's domestic program, later termed the Fair Deal. The reaction from Congress, however, was hostile. By 1946, nearly 2,000,000 people were unemployed, consumers were striking, and labor unions were striking for higher wages. Truman's determination to prevent strikes led to frequent confrontations with John L. Lewis (1880–1969), head of the United Mine Workers, and other labor leaders. In May, 1946, the tough, straight-talking Truman told leaders of railroad workers' unions threatening a strike, "If you think I'm going to sit here and let you tie up this whole country, you're crazy as hell." He then revealed plans to draft strikers into the army and force

UPI

Truman played the piano for the Kennedys at 1961 White House dinner.

them to run the trains. The railroad men did not strike. Truman, however, did not favor legislative curbs on labor and vetoed the antilabor Case Bill in 1946 and the somewhat milder **Taft-Hartley Act** (*see*) in 1947. Truman's actions nevertheless alienated labor, which did not like his toughness. Moreover, businesses did not like his position on price controls, the South was antagonized by his civil-rights proposals, and the North did not like his plainspoken forthrightness. Admittedly corny, the President once entertained foreign dignitaries by playing the "Missouri Waltz" on the piano. His references to his wife, Bess (born 1885), as "the Boss" and his blunt letters to critics who gave bad reviews to his daughter, Margaret (born 1924), a singer, seemed to many to be beneath the dignity of his office. The Congressional elections of 1946 produced the first Republican-controlled Congress since 1930. Meanwhile, Truman's attention became increasingly occupied with foreign affairs. The basic idea behind his foreign policy—the so-called **Truman Doctrine** (*see*)—was the containment of Communism, and early in 1947 he asked Congress to appropriate money to aid Greece and Turkey in their struggle against Com-

munism. This was followed by the implementation of the Marshall Plan, which involved spending billions of American dollars to rebuild Western Europe. Russia challenged Truman by blocking Allied access to Berlin in June, 1948. Truman responded with the **Berlin Airlift** (*see*), forcing the Soviets to back down. Truman's decision, in 1948, to seek his own four-year term was not a popular one, even within his own party. Left-wing Democrats organized a third party and nominated Henry A. Wallace (1888–1965) for President. The South bolted when Truman insisted on a civil-rights plank in the platform and nominated Strom Thurmond (born 1902) on a states' rights ticket. The remaining Democrats lamely nominated Truman and chose Senator Alben W. Barkley (1877–1956) of Kentucky as his running mate. Truman immediately called the Republican-dominated 80th Congress back in session, and when it refused to pass the laws he wanted he labeled it the "do-nothing" Congress and blamed it for many of the nation's ills. During his whistle-stop campaign, the crowds frequently shouted, "Give 'em hell, Harry!" The polls, however, forecast a landslide victory for Republican **Thomas E. Dewey** (*see*). In his astounding upset victory, Truman won the labor and farm vote and polled 303 electoral votes to Dewey's 189. Thurmond received 39. Truman's popular vote exceeded 24,000,-000, and his plurality was over 2,000,000. The Democrats also gained control of Congress. Many of Truman's Fair Deal proposals—in the fields of low-rent public housing, minimum-wage legislation, Social Security benefits, and rent control—were enacted into law during his second administration. He also desegregated the armed forces by executive order. However, most of his time was spent on foreign affairs. The **North Atlantic Treaty Organization** (*see*) was established in 1949 to resist possible Communist aggression in Europe, a menace that loomed large after the Russians exploded an atomic bomb that year and China fell to Communists led by Mao Tse-tung (born 1893). In 1950, the Point Four Program, designed to aid economically underdeveloped countries, was launched. Meanwhile, the House Un-American Activities Committee, which Truman called "the most un-American activity in the whole government," had started a search for Communists in America that was later exploited by Senator **Joseph R. McCarthy** (*see*) of Wisconsin. The case of **Alger Hiss** (*see*), a former State Department employee accused of being a Communist agent, and the **Rosenberg spy case** (*see*), involving the sale of atomic secrets to Russia, heightened the hysteria. The McCarran Internal Security Act, passed over Truman's veto in September, 1950, required all members of the Communist Party and of Communist-front organizations to register with the Attorney General. It also prohibited aliens who had been Communists from entering the country, barred the employment of Communists in defense plants, and authorized the President to hold them in detention camps in the event of war. Truman believed the act was unconstitutional, and the Supreme Court ruled, in 1965, that the registration provision was unconstitutional. On June 25, 1950, North Korean troops invaded South Korea. Truman immediately sent troops to Korea and appealed to the United Nations for support. The Security Council voted for intervention and asked Truman to appoint a commanding officer.

He chose General Douglas MacArthur (1880–1964). By April, 1951, MacArthur, who believed in attacking China itself, had made a number of public statements critical of the administration's war policy, especially Truman's insistence on limiting the fighting to Korea. In one of his most difficult and controversial decisions, the President reasserted civilian control over the military by relieving MacArthur of command. Later, Truman explained, "General MacArthur was insubordinate and I fired him. That's all there was to it." On November 1, 1950, two Puerto Rican nationalists tried to assassinate Truman at Blair House, where he was living while the White House, across the street, was being renovated. Truman was not injured, but a Secret Serviceman and one of the assailants were killed. The surviving one was sentenced to death, but Truman commuted the sentence to life imprisonment. In March, 1952, Truman announced that he would not be a candidate for reelection and, shortly afterward, indicated that his choice for the Democratic nomination was **Adlai E. Stevenson** (*see*) of Illinois. In January, 1953, Truman returned to his home in Independence, Missouri. There he founded the Truman Library, (1957). He published three volumes of memoirs, *Years of Decision* (1955), *Years of Trial and Hope* (1956), and *Mr. Citizen* (1960).

TRUMAN DOCTRINE. As the first step of his program to contain the influence of communism, President **Harry S. Truman** (*see*) told a joint session of Congress on March 12, 1947, "I believe that it must be the policy of the United States to support free peoples who are resisting attempted subjugation by armed

minorities or by outside pressures. I believe that we must assist free peoples to work out their own destinies in their own way." This bold foreign policy statement has since been called the Truman Doctrine. The President's request for $400,000,000 to assist Greece and Turkey in resisting communism was passed by Congress on May 22 after considerable debate. Initially, the Truman Doctrine was restricted to nations where there was danger of a Communist take-over. However, on June 5, 1947, in a commencement address at Harvard, Secretary of State George C. Marshall (1880–1959) warned that a stable European economy was essential to America's security. He suggested that U.S. policy should be directed against "hunger, poverty, desperation, and chaos. Its purpose should be the revival of a working economy in the world." Thus, the European Recovery Program, or Marshall Plan, became an extension of the Truman Doctrine, offering American aid to all nations that desired to rebuild their economy, including the Soviet Union and other Communist countries. Russia immediately denounced the Marshall Plan on the ground that it would entail meddling in internal affairs, and none of the Soviet-dominated Eastern European countries participated. On the other hand, France and Great Britain voiced approval and asked interested countries to meet in Paris to estimate their needs and to formulate a program. Sixteen nations attended the initial conference: Britain, France, Austria, Belgium, Denmark, Greece, Iceland, Ireland, Italy, Luxembourg, the Netherlands, Norway, Portugal, Sweden, Switzerland, and Turkey. They estimated that with $19,300,000,000 from America and an additional $3,100,000,000 from the International Bank they could achieve stability and self-sufficiency by 1951. In December, Truman recommended that Congress appropriate $17,000,-000,000 to be spent over a five-year period to ensure the permanent recovery of Europe's economy. A Communist coup in Czechoslovakia in February, 1948, sped the passage of the administration's bill. That April, the European Cooperation Administration was established to promote Europe's production and to bolster its currency as well as to facilitate international trade. Within three years, America spent more than $12,000,-000,000, and a thriving Western Europe proved a formidable barrier against further Communist gains. The Point Four Program was an additional step by Truman to contain communism. As the fourth point on foreign policy in his inaugural address on January 20, 1949, Truman proposed a program aimed at lending technical assistance to underdeveloped countries. The initial appropriation was passed by Congress in September, 1950, after the outbreak of the Korean war. Eventually, 54 nations took advantage of the program, which was administered by the Technical Cooperation Administration. Under President **Dwight D. Eisenhower** (*see*) the program was integrated into the overall foreign-aid program.

VOTING RIGHTS ACT OF 1965. *See* **Civil-rights Movement.**

WALLACE, George Corley (born 1919). A leading Southern segregationist and advocate of states' rights, Wallace was born and raised on a farm in Clio, Alabama. While in high school, he won a state bantamweight boxing championship. He worked his way through the University of Alabama Law School by boxing professionally, waiting on tables, and driving a taxi. After receiving his law degree in 1942, Wallace joined the army air force. He served as a flight engineer on a B-29 in the Pacific during World War II. In 1946, Wallace became an assistant attorney general of Alabama. The following year, he was elected to the first of two terms in the state legislature and was active in encouraging new industry into Alabama and training skilled labor. Despite his opposition to a strong civil-rights platform at the 1948 Democratic National Convention, Wallace refused to walk out of the convention with Governor Strom Thurmond (born 1902) of South Carolina and other so-called Dixiecrats. Elected to the third judicial circuit in 1953, he soon gained a reputation as the "fighting judge" because of his defiance of federal efforts to open voter-registration rolls to Negroes. After losing the Democratic primary contest for governor in 1958 to a militant segregationist, Wallace determined not to be "out-segged" again. He campaigned for the nomination again in 1962 like "a one-man army at war with the Federal Government." Promising that he would personally block any attempt to desegregate Alabama public schools, Wallace won the primary and then the election. In June, 1963, he kept his campaign pledge by barring the path of two Negroes trying to register at the University of Alabama. It was only after President **John F. Kennedy** (*see*) federalized the Alabama National Guard and sent several units to the campus that Wallace backed down. Kennedy had to federalize the state guardsmen again that September in order to force the integration of public schools throughout the state. Wallace announced his candidacy for the Presidency on a third-party ticket in 1964 but withdrew in favor of **Barry M. Goldwater** (*see*) of Arizona, a conservative who had won the Republican nomination. With Curtis LeMay (born 1906), the former commander of the Strategic Air Command, as his running mate, Wallace did run for the Presidency in 1968. He hoped to capture enough electoral votes in the South to create a deadlock between Republican **Richard M. Nixon** and Democrat **Hubert H. Humphrey** (*see both*). Such a deadlock would have thrown the election into the House for the first time since 1824, when John Quincy Adams (1767–1848) was chosen President, although Andrew Jackson (1767–1845) had received more popular and electoral votes. Wallace believed that he could either win the Presidency in the same manner or force either Nixon or Humphrey to bargain with him for his votes. Although Wallace received more than 10,000,000 popular votes nationally, he gained only 46 electoral votes—those of Alabama, Arkansas, Georgia, Louisiana, and Mississippi. Nixon, meanwhile, won the election with 301 electoral votes to Humphrey's 191. Although barred under Alabama law from holding two consecutive terms, Wallace in effect ruled as governor through his wife, Lurleen Burns Wallace (1927–1968), who won the governorship in 1966. His campaign for the Presidency two years later was financed with state funds. Even after his wife's death from cancer, Wallace continued to exercise a dominating role in Alabama politics. He was re-elected governor in 1970.

WARREN, Earl (born 1891). As the Chief Justice of the United States for 16 years (1953–1969), Warren presided over the Supreme Court during one of the most active and controversial periods in its history. Under his leadership, the Court abandoned the relatively passive role it had frequently played in the past to assume equal status with the Presidency and the Congress in the government of the United States. Warren was born in Los Angeles. As a high-school student in Kern County, California, he resolved to become a lawyer after viewing criminal trials at the county courthouse. Warren majored in political science while attending the University of California at Berkeley. In 1914, he was admitted to the California bar shortly after receiving a Doctor of Laws degree from Berkeley. Warren served as a corporation lawyer before joining the army in 1917 as a private. He was a training instructor until his discharge in late 1918 as a first lieutenant. Warren was an assistant to the Oakland city attorney from 1919 to 1920. He was then appointed a deputy to the district attorney of Alameda County. In 1925, Warren became the district attorney, a post he held for 13 years. In 1938, he was elected attorney general of California after winning nomination by three parties—Republican, Democratic, and Progressive. Warren was notably successful in combating illegal gambling and racketeering, but he was criticized for approving the removal of many Nisei (Japanese-Americans) to relocation centers during World War II. Running as a Republican, Warren was elected governor of California in 1942. He was reelected in 1946 and 1950, becoming the state's only chief executive to serve three consecutive terms.

As governor, Warren conducted a largely nonpartisan administration. He instituted many social-welfare programs and backed legislation that reduced state sales taxes and provided funds for the development of California. Warren was the keynote speaker at the Republican National Convention in 1944, and he was nominated for President as California's "favorite son" candidate. Four years later, Warren, an announced contender for the Presidency, withdrew from the race and swung his crucial support to **Thomas E. Dewey** (*see*). He subsequently accepted Dewey's invitation to run as the Republican Vice-Presidential candidate. However, the Dewey-Warren slate was defeated by a Democratic ticket headed by President **Harry S. Truman** (*see*). In 1952, Warren again commanded a substantial following at the Republican National Convention, but the nomination and the subsequent general election were won by **Dwight D. Eisenhower** (*see*). On September 30, 1953, Eisenhower appointed Warren Chief Justice of the Supreme Court to succeed the late Frederick M. Vinson (1890–1953). Warren viewed the Court as an agency of moderation. "I conceive of this Court," he said, "as the balance wheel of this government. Its function is to keep us from swinging too violently to one extreme or another." However, the "Warren Court," as it came to be called, was soon characterized, by friends and critics alike, as one of the most liberal in the nation's history. On May 17, 1954, in a landmark opinion written by the Chief Justice, it ruled in *Brown vs. Board of Education of Topeka, Kansas* that racial segregation in public schools was unconstitutional. This decision overturned the "separate but equal" doctrine

established by the Supreme Court in 1896 and was largely responsible for generating the **Civil-rights Movement** (*see*) of the 1950s and 60s. Other important Warren Court rulings included *Reynolds vs. Sims* (1963), which directed that the membership of state legislatures be determined by the "one-man, one-vote" principle, and *Miranda vs. Arizona* (1965), which established that a citizen held in custody by the police must be informed of his right to an attorney and his right to refrain from incriminating himself. These important opinions were written by Warren, as was the decision in *Powell vs. McCormack* (1969), in which the Court decided that New York Representative Adam Clayton Powell, Jr. (born 1908) had been illegally excluded from his seat in the House of Representatives in 1967. Retiring to private life on June 23, 1969, Warren was praised by President **Richard M. Nixon** (*see*)—a former political foe of Warren's—for his integrity, fairness, and dignity. He was succeeded as Chief Justice by Warren E. Burger (born 1908).

UPI

Earl Warren (left) with the President after Warren E. Burger (right) was sworn in as new Chief Justice.

ELECTION YEAR	PRESIDENT	PARTY	ELECTORAL VOTE
1788	George Washington		69
1792	George Washington		132
1796	John Adams	Federalist	71
1800	Thomas Jefferson	Democratic–Republican	73
1804	Thomas Jefferson	Democratic–Republican	162
1808	James Madison	Democratic–Republican	122
1812	James Madison	Democratic–Republican	128
1816	James Monroe	Democratic–Republican	183
1820	James Monroe	Democratic–Republican	231
1824	John Quincy Adams[1]	National Republican	84
1828	Andrew Jackson	Democratic	178
1832	Andrew Jackson	Democratic	219
1836	Martin Van Buren	Democratic	170
1840	William Henry Harrison	Whig	234
	John Tyler*	Whig	
1844	James K. Polk	Democratic	170
1848	Zachary Taylor	Whig	163
	Millard Fillmore*	Whig	
1852	Franklin Pierce	Democratic	254
1856	James Buchanan	Democratic	174
1860	Abraham Lincoln	Republican	180
1864	Abraham Lincoln	Republican	212
	Andrew Johnson*	Republican	
1868	Ulysses S. Grant	Republican	214
1872	Ulysses S. Grant	Republican	286
1876	Rutherford B. Hayes	Republican	185
1880	James A. Garfield	Republican	214
	Chester A. Arthur*	Republican	
1884	Grover Cleveland	Democratic	219
1888	Benjamin Harrison	Republican	233
1892	Grover Cleveland	Democratic	277
1896	William McKinley	Republican	271
1900	William McKinley	Republican	292
	Theodore Roosevelt*	Republican	
1904	Theodore Roosevelt	Republican	336
1908	William H. Taft	Republican	321
1912	Woodrow Wilson	Democratic	435
1916	Woodrow Wilson	Democratic	277
1920	Warren G. Harding	Republican	404
	Calvin Coolidge*	Republican	
1924	Calvin Coolidge	Republican	382
1928	Herbert Hoover	Republican	444
1932	Franklin D. Roosevelt	Democratic	472
1936	Franklin D. Roosevelt	Democratic	523
1940	Franklin D. Roosevelt	Democratic	449
1944	Franklin D. Roosevelt	Democratic	432
	Harry S. Truman*	Democratic	
1948	Harry S. Truman	Democratic	303
1952	Dwight D. Eisenhower	Republican	442
1956	Dwight D. Eisenhower	Republican	457
1960	John F. Kennedy	Democratic	303
	Lyndon B. Johnson*	Democratic	
1964	Lyndon B. Johnson	Democratic	486
1968	Richard M. Nixon	Republican	301

*Vice-President who succeeded to the office of the elected President and completed his term.

[1]No one of the four candidates received a majority of the electoral votes, so the House of Representatives decided the election.

PRESIDENTIAL ELECTIONS

PRINCIPAL OPPONENT	PARTY	ELECTORAL VOTE	NUMBER OF STATES
(No opponent)		...	11
(No opponent)		...	15
Thomas Jefferson	Democratic–Republican	68	16
John Adams	Federalist	65	16
C. C. Pinckney	Federalist	14	17
C. C. Pinckney	Federalist	47	17
DeWitt Clinton	Federalist	89	18
Rufus King	Federalist	34	19
(No opponent)		...	24
Andrew Jackson	Democratic	99	24
John Quincy Adams	National Republican	83	24
Henry Clay	Whig	49	25
William H. Harrison	Whig	73	26
Martin Van Buren	Democratic	60	26
Henry Clay	Whig	105	26
Lewis Cass	Democratic	127	30
Winfield Scott	Whig	42	31
John C. Fremont	Republican	114	31
John C. Breckenridge	Democratic	72	33
George B. McClellan	Democratic	21	36
Horatio Seymour	Democratic	80	37
Horace Greeley [2]	Liberal Republican–Democratic	...	37
Samuel J. Tilden	Democratic	184	38
Winfield S. Hancock	Democratic	155	38
James G. Blaine	Republican	182	38
Grover Cleveland	Democratic	168	38
Benjamin Harrison	Republican	145	44
William J. Bryan	Democratic	176	45
William J. Bryan	Democratic	155	45
Alton B. Parker	Democratic	140	45
William J. Bryan	Democratic	162	46
Theodore Roosevelt	Progressive	88	48
Charles E. Hughes	Republican	254	48
James M. Cox	Democratic	127	48
John W. Davis	Democratic	136	48
Alfred E. Smith	Democratic	87	48
Herbert Hoover	Republican	59	48
Alfred M. Landon	Republican	8	48
Wendell L. Willkie	Republican	82	48
Thomas E. Dewey	Republican	99	48
Thomas E. Dewey	Republican	189	48
Adlai E. Stevenson	Democratic	89	48
Adlai E. Stevenson	Democratic	73	48
Richard M. Nixon	Republican	219	50
Barry M. Goldwater	Republican	52	50
Hubert H. Humphrey	Democratic	191	50

[2] Because of Greeley's death before the electoral college met, the electors representing those who had voted for him cast their votes for other candidates.

THE PRESIDENTS AND THEIR CABINETS

PRESIDENT AND VICE-PRESIDENT	SECRETARY OF STATE	SECRETARY OF THE TREASURY	SECRETARY OF WAR
George Washington–John Adams 1789	Thomas Jefferson . . 1789 Edmund Randolph . 1794 Timothy Pickering . 1795	Alex. Hamilton . . . . 1789 Oliver Wolcott 1795	Henry Knox . . . . 1789 Timothy Pickering . 1795 James McHenry . . . 1796
John Adams–Thomas Jefferson 1797	Timothy Pickering . 1797 John Marshall 1800	Oliver Wolcott . . . . . 1797 Samuel Dexter 1801	James McHenry . . . 1797 John Marshall . . . . . 1800 Samuel Dexter . . . . . 1800 Roger Griswold 1801
Thomas Jefferson–Aaron Burr . . . . 1801 George Clinton 1805	James Madison 1801	Samuel Dexter . . . . . 1801 Albert Gallatin 1801	Henry Dearborn . . . 1801
James Madison–George Clinton . . . . 1809 Elbridge Gerry 1813	Robert Smith . . . . . . 1809 James Monroe 1811	Albert Gallatin . . . . 1809 G. W. Campbell . . . 1814 A. J. Dallas . . . . 1814 Wm. H. Crawford . . 1816	William Eustis . . . . . 1809 John Armstrong . . . 1813 James Monroe . . . . . 1814 Wm. H. Crawford . . 1815
James Monroe–Daniel D. Tompkins 1817	John Q. Adams 1817	Wm. H. Crawford . . 1817	Isaac Shelby . . . . 1817 George Graham . . . 1817 John C. Calhoun . . . 1817
John Quincy Adams–John C. Calhoun 1825	Henry Clay 1825	Richard Rush 1825	James Barbour . . . . . 1825 Peter B. Porter 1828
Andrew Jackson–John C. Calhoun . . . . 1829 Martin Van Buren 1833	Martin Van Buren . . 1829 Edward Livingston . 1831 Louis McLane . . . . . 1833 John Forsyth 1834	Samuel D. Ingham . 1829 Louis McLane . . . . . 1831 William J. Duane . . 1833 Roger B. Taney . . . . 1833 Levi Woodbury 1834	John H. Eaton . . . . . 1829 Lewis Cass . . . . 1831 Benjamin F. Butler . 1837
Martin Van Buren–Richard M. Johnson 1837	John Forsyth 1837	Levi Woodbury 1837	Joel R. Poinsett 1837
William H. Harrison–John Tyler 1841	Daniel Webster 1841	Thomas Ewing 1841	John Bell 1841
John Tyler 1841	Daniel Webster . . . . 1841 Hugh S. Legare . . . . 1843 Abel P. Upshur . . . . 1843 John C. Calhoun . . . 1844	Thomas Ewing . . . . . 1841 Walter Forward . . . . 1841 John C. Spencer . . . . 1843 George M. Bibb 1844	John Bell . . . . 1841 John McLean . . . . . . 1841 John C. Spencer . . . . 1841 James M. Porter . . . 1843 William Wilkins . . . 1844
James K. Polk–George M. Dallas 1845	James Buchanan . . . 1845	Robert J. Walker . . . 1845	William L. Marcy . . 1845
Zachary Taylor–Millard Fillmore 1849	John M. Clayton . . . 1849	Wm. M. Meredith . . 1849	Geo. W. Crawford . 1849
Millard Fillmore 1850	Daniel Webster . . . . 1850 Edward Everett 1852	Thomas Corwin 1850	Charles M. Conrad . 1850
Franklin Pierce–William R. King 1853	William L. Marcy . . 1853	James Guthrie 1853	Jefferson Davis 1853
James Buchanan–John C. Breckinridge 1857	Lewis Cass . . . . 1857 Jeremiah S. Black . . 1860	Howell Cobb . . . . . . 1857 Philip F. Thomas . . . 1860 John A. Dix 1861	John B. Floyd . . . . . 1857 Joseph Holt 1861
Abraham Lincoln–Hannibal Hamlin . . . . 1861 Andrew Johnson 1865	William H. Seward . 1861	Salmon P. Chase . . . 1861 Wm. P. Fessenden . . 1864 Hugh McCulloch . . 1865	Simon Cameron . . . 1861 Edwin M. Stanton . . 1862
Andrew Johnson 1865	William H. Seward . 1865	Hugh McCulloch . . 1865	Edwin M. Stanton . . 1865 Ulysses S. Grant . . . 1867 Lorenzo Thomas . . . 1868 John M. Schofield . . 1868

SECRETARY OF THE NAVY	SECRETARY OF THE INTERIOR	POSTMASTER GENERAL	ATTORNEY GENERAL	OTHER MEMBERS
	Established March 3, 1849	Samuel Osgood .... 1789 Timothy Pickering . 1791 Joseph Habersham . 1795	Edmund Randolph . 1789 William Bradford . . 1794 Charles Lee 1795	**SECRETARY OF AGRICULTURE**
Benjamin Stoddert. . 1798		Joseph Habersham . 1797	Charles Lee .... 1797 Theophilus Parsons. 1801	Established February 11, 1889 Norman J. Colman .... 1889 Jeremiah M. Rusk ..... 1889 J. Sterling Morton ..... 1893 James Wilson......... 1897
Benjamin Stoddert. . 1801 Robert Smith ...... 1801 J. Crowninshield ... 1805		Joseph Habersham . 1801 Gideon Granger ... 1801	Levi Lincoln....... 1801 Robert Smith ...... 1805 John Breckinridge. . 1805 Caesar A. Rodney . . 1807	James Wilson......... 1901 James Wilson......... 1909 David F. Houston ..... 1913 Edward T. Meredith ... 1920
Paul Hamilton ..... 1809 William Jones ..... 1813 B.W.Crowninshield 1814		Gideon Granger ... 1809 Return J. Meigs, Jr.. 1814	Caesar A. Rodney . 1809 William Pinckney . . 1811 Richard Rush 1814	Henry C. Wallace ..... 1921 Howard M. Gore...... 1924 William M. Jardine .... 1925 Arthur M. Hyde....... 1929
B.W.Crowninshield 1817 Smith Thompson... 1818 S. L. Southard 1823		Return J. Meigs, Jr.. 1817 John McLean...... 1823	Richard Rush ..... 1817 William Wirt 1817	Henry A. Wallace ..... 1933 Claude R. Wickard .... 1940 Clinton P. Anderson ... 1945 Charles F. Brannan 1948
S. L. Southard 1825		John McLean...... 1825	William Wirt 1825	Ezra Taft Benson ...... 1953 Orville L. Freeman .... 1961 Clifford M. Hardin..... 1969
John Branch....... 1829 Levi Woodbury .... 1831 Mahlon Dickerson . 1834		William T. Barry... 1829 Amos Kendall 1835	John M. Berrien ... 1829 Roger B. Taney .... 1831 Benjamin F. Butler . 1833	**SECRETARY OF COMMERCE AND LABOR** Established February 14, 1903
Mahlon Dickerson . 1837 James K. Paulding. . 1838		Amos Kendall ..... 1837 John M. Niles 1840	Benjamin F. Butler . 1837 Felix Grundy ...... 1838 Henry D. Gilpin ... 1840	George B. Cortelyou ... 1903 Victor H. Metcalf...... 1904 Oscar S. Straus........ 1906
George E. Badger .. 1841		Francis Granger ... 1841	John J. Crittenden. . 1841	Charles Nagel......... 1909
George E. Badger .. 1841 Abel P. Upshur .... 1841 David Henshaw.... 1843 Thomas W. Gilmer . 1844 John Y. Mason 1844		Francis Granger ... 1841 Chas. A. Wickliffe. . 1841	John J. Crittenden. . 1841 Hugh S. Legare .... 1841 John Nelson....... 1843	**SECRETARY OF COMMERCE†**
George Bancroft ... 1845 John Y. Mason 1846		Cave Johnson 1845	John Y. Mason .... 1845 Nathan Clifford.... 1846 Isaac Toucey 1848	William C. Redfield .... 1913 Joshua W. Alexander ... 1919 Herbert Hoover .... 1921 Herbert Hoover .... 1925 William F. Whiting.... 1928
William B. Preston . 1849	Thomas Ewing..... 1849	Jacob Collamer 1849	Reverdy Johnson... 1849	Robert P. Lamont...... 1929 Roy D. Chapin 1932
Wm. A. Graham ... 1850 John P. Kennedy ... 1852	Alex. H. H. Stuart. . 1850	Nathan K. Hall .... 1850 Sam. D. Hubbard .. 1852	John J. Crittenden. . 1850	Daniel C. Roper .... 1933 Harry L. Hopkins...... 1939 Jesse Jones............ 1940
James C. Dobbin... 1853	Robert McClelland . 1853	James Campbell ... 1853	Caleb Cushing 1853	Henry A. Wallace 1945
Isaac Toucey 1857	Jacob Thompson... 1857	Aaron V. Brown ... 1857 Joseph Holt 1859	Jeremiah S. Black .. 1857 Edwin M. Stanton. . 1860	W. A. Harriman .... 1946 Charles Sawyer .... 1948 Sinclair Weeks........ 1953 Luther Hodges 1961
Gideon Welles 1861	Caleb B. Smith..... 1861 John P. Usher 1863	Horatio King...... 1861 Montgomery Blair . 1861 William Dennison. . 1864	Edward Bates...... 1861 Titian J. Coffey .... 1863 James Speed....... 1864	John T. Connor........ 1965 Alexander Trow- bridge.............. 1967
Gideon Welles 1865	John P. Usher ..... 1865 James Harlan...... 1865 O. H. Browning.... 1866	William Dennison. . 1865 Alex. W. Randall... 1866	James Speed....... 1865 Henry Stanbery .... 1866 William M. Evarts. . 1868	C. R. Smith .... 1968 Maurice H. Stans 1969

PRESIDENT AND VICE-PRESIDENT	SECRETARY OF STATE	SECRETARY OF THE TREASURY	SECRETARY OF WAR
Ulysses S. Grant–Schuyler Colfax . . . . 1869 Henry Wilson 1873	E. B. Washburne . . . 1869 Hamilton Fish 1869	George S. Boutwell . 1869 W. A. Richardson . . 1873 Benj. H. Bristow . . . 1874 Lot M. Morrill 1876	John A. Rawlins . . . 1869 W. T. Sherman . . . . 1869 Wm. W. Belknap . . . 1869 Alphonso Taft . . . . . 1876 James D. Cameron . 1876
Rutherford B. Hayes–William A. Wheeler 1877	William M. Evarts . 1877	John Sherman 1877	Geo. W. McCrary . . 1877 Alexander Ramsey . 1879
James A. Garfield–Chester A. Arthur 1881	James G. Blaine 1881	William Windom . . . 1881	Robert T. Lincoln . . 1881
Chester A. Arthur 1881	Frederick T. Freling- huysen 1881	Charles J. Folger . . . 1881 Walter Q. Gresham . 1884 Hugh McCulloch . . 1884	Robert T. Lincoln . . 1881
Grover Cleveland–Thomas A. Hendricks 1885	Thomas F. Bayard . 1885	Daniel Manning . . . 1885 Chas. S. Fairchild . . 1887	Wm. C. Endicott . . . 1885
Benjamin Harrison–Levi P. Morton 1889	James G. Blaine . . . . 1889 John W. Foster 1892	William Windom . . . 1889 Charles Foster 1891	Redfield Proctor . . . 1889 Stephen B. Elkins . . 1891
Grover Cleveland–Adlai E. Stevenson 1893	Walter Q. Gresham . 1893 Richard Olney 1895	John G. Carlisle . . . 1893	Daniel S. Lamont . . 1893
William McKinley–Garret A. Hobart . . . . 1897 Theodore Roosevelt 1901	John Sherman . . . . . 1897 William R. Day . . . . 1897 John Hay 1898	Lyman J. Gage 1897	Russell A. Alger . . . 1897 Elihu Root 1899
Theodore Roosevelt . . . . 1901 Charles W. Fairbanks 1905	John Hay . . . . 1901 Elihu Root . . . . 1905 Robert Bacon 1909	Lyman J. Gage . . . . 1901 Leslie M. Shaw . . . . 1902 Geo. B. Cortelyou . . 1907	Elihu Root . . . . 1901 William H. Taft . . . . 1904 Luke E. Wright 1908
William H. Taft–James S. Sherman 1909	Philander C. Knox . 1909	Fkln. MacVeagh . . . 1909	J. M. Dickinson . . . . 1909 Henry L. Stimson . . 1911
Woodrow Wilson–Thomas R. Marshall 1913	William J. Bryan . . . 1913 Robert Lansing . . . . 1915 Bainbridge Colby . . 1920	Wm. G. McAdoo . . 1913 Carter Glass . . . . . . 1919 David F. Houston . . 1929	L. M. Garrison . . . . 1913 Newton D. Baker . . 1916
Warren G. Harding–Calvin Coolidge 1921	Charles E. Hughes . . 1921	Andrew W. Mellon . 1921	John W. Weeks 1921
Calvin Coolidge . . . . 1923 Charles G. Dawes 1925	Charles E. Hughes . 1923 Frank B. Kellogg . . . 1925	Andrew W. Mellon . 1923	John W. Weeks . . . . 1923 Dwight F. Davis . . . 1925
Herbert C. Hoover–Charles Curtis 1929	Henry L. Stimson . . 1929	Andrew W. Mellon . 1929 Ogden L. Mills 1932	James W. Good . . . . 1929 Patrick J. Hurley . . . 1929
Franklin Delano Roosevelt–John Nance Garner . . . . . 1933 Henry A. Wallace . . . . 1941 Harry S. Truman 1945	Cordell Hull . . . . 1933 Edward R. Stettinius, Jr. 1944	Wm. H. Woodin . . . 1933 Henry Morgenthau, Jr. 1934	George H. Dern . . . 1933 H. A. Woodring . . . 1936 Henry L. Stimson . . 1940
Harry S. Truman . . . . 1945 Alben W. Barkley 1949	James F. Byrnes . . . . 1945 Geo. C. Marshall . . 1947 Dean Acheson 1949	Fred M. Vinson . . . . 1945 John W. Snyder 1946	Robt. P. Patterson . . 1945 Ken. C. Royall 1947*
Dwight D. Eisenhower–Richard M. Nixon 1953	John F. Dulles . . . . . 1953 Christian A. Herter . 1959	G. M. Humphrey . . 1953 Robt. B. Anderson . 1957	
John F. Kennedy–Lyndon B. Johnson 1961	Dean Rusk 1961	C. Douglas Dillon . . 1961	
Lyndon B. Johnson . . . . 1963 Hubert H. Humphrey . . . . 1965 Richard M. Nixon–Spiro T. Agnew 1969	Dean Rusk . . . . 1963 William P. Rogers . . 1969	C. Douglas Dillon . . 1963 Henry H. Fowler . . . 1965 Joseph W. Barr . . . . 1968 David M. Kennedy . 1969 John B. Connally . . . 1970	

*On July 26, 1947, the Department of War and the Department of the Navy were combined into a newly established Department of Defense.

SECRETARY OF THE NAVY	SECRETARY OF THE INTERIOR	POSTMASTER GENERAL	ATTORNEY GENERAL	OTHER MEMBERS
Adolph E. Borie.... 1869 Geo. M. Robeson .. 1869	Jacob D. Cox...... 1869 Columbus Delano.. 1870 Zach. Chandler 1875	John A. J. Creswell . 1869 James W. Marshall . 1874 Marshall Jewell .... 1874 James N. Tyner 1876	Ebenezer R. Hoar .. 1869 Amos T. Ackerman. 1870 Geo. H. Williams .. 1871 Edw. Pierrepont ... 1875 Alphonso Taft 1876	**SECRETARY OF LABOR†** Established March 4, 1913 William B. Wilson..... 1913
R. W. Thompson.... 1877 Nathan Goff, Jr. ... 1881	Carl Schurz 1877	David M. Key ..... 1877 Horace Maynard... 1880	Charles Devens 1877	James J. Davis .... 1921 James J. Davis .... 1923 James J. Davis 1929
William H. Hunt ... 1881	Sam. J. Kirkwood .. 1881	Thomas L. James .. 1881	Wayne MacVeagh .. 1881	William N. Doak...... 1930
Wm. E. Chandler... 1881	Henry M. Teller.... 1881	Timothy O. Howe .. 1881 Walter Q. Gresham. 1883 Frank Hatton 1884	Benj. H. Brewster .. 1881	Frances Perkins .... 1933 L. B. Schwellenbach ... 1945 Maurice J. Tobin.... 1948 Martin P. Durkin..... 1953
William C. Whitney 1885	L. Q. C. Lamar .... 1885 William F. Vilas ... 1888	William F. Vilas ... 1885 Don M. Dickinson . 1888	A. H. Garland 1885	James P. Mitchell...... 1953 Arthur J. Goldberg 1961
Benjamin F. Tracy.. 1889	John W. Noble 1889	John Wanamaker .. 1889	Wm. H. H. Miller .. 1889	W. Willard Wirtz...... 1962 George P. Shultz ...... 1969 James D. Hodgson 1970
Hilary A. Herbert .. 1893	Hoke Smith .... 1893 David R. Francis... 1896	Wilson S. Bissell ... 1893 William L. Wilson.. 1895	Richard Olney ..... 1893 Judson Harmon.... 1895	**SECRETARY OF DEFENSE** Established July 26, 1947
John D. Long...... 1897	Cornelius N. Bliss .. 1897 E. A. Hitchcock.... 1899	James A. Gary..... 1897 Charles E. Smith ... 1898	Joseph McKenna... 1897 John W. Griggs .... 1897 Philander C. Knox . 1901	James V. Forrestal..... 1947 Louis A. Johnson...... 1949
John D. Long...... 1901 William H. Moody . 1902 Paul Morton ...... 1904 Chas. J. Bonaparte . 1905 Victor H. Metcalf .. 1907 T. H. Newberry 1908	E. A. Hitchcock.... 1901 James R. Garfield .. 1907	Charles E. Smith ... 1901 Henry C. Payne.... 1902 Robert J. Wynne ... 1904 Geo. B. Cortelyou . 1905 Geo. von L. Meyer . 1907	Philander C. Knox . 1901 William H. Moody . 1904 Chas. J. Bonaparte . 1907	George C. Marshall.... 1950 Robert A. Lovett ...... 1951 Charles E. Wilson ..... 1953 Neil H. McElroy ...... 1957 Thomas S. Gates, Jr. ... 1959 Robert S. McNamara . 1961
Geo. von L. Meyer . 1909	R. A. Ballinger .... 1909 Walter L. Fisher ... 1911	F. H. Hitchcock.... 1909	G. W. Wickersham . 1909	Clark M. Clifford ...... 1968 Melvin R. Laird 1969
Josephus Daniels ... 1913	Franklin K. Lane .. 1913 John B. Payne 1920	Albert S. Burleson.. 1913	J. C. McReynolds .. 1913 Thos. W. Gregory .. 1914 A. Mitchell Palmer . 1919	**SECRETARY OF HEALTH, EDUCATION, AND WELFARE** Established April 1, 1953
Edwin Denby...... 1921	Albert B. Fall...... 1921 Hubert Work...... 1923	Will H. Hays ...... 1921 Hubert Work...... 1922 Harry S. New...... 1923	H. M. Daugherty... 1921	Oveta Culp Hobby..... 1953 Marion B. Folsom 1955
Edwin Denby...... 1923 Curtis D. Wilbur ... 1924	Hubert Work...... 1923 Roy O. West 1928	Harry S. New...... 1923	H. M. Daugherty... 1923 Harlan F. Stone.... 1924 John G. Sargent.... 1925	Arthur S. Flemming... 1958 Abraham A. Ribicoff... 1961 Anthony J. Celebrezze.. 1962
Charles F. Adams .. 1929	Ray L. Wilbur 1929	Walter F. Brown ... 1929	Wm. D. Mitchell ... 1929	John W. Gardner ...... 1965 Wilbur J. Cohen .... 1968 Robert H. Finch 1969
Claude A. Swanson . 1933 Charles Edison..... 1940 Frank Knox 1940	Harold L. Ickes 1933	James A. Farley.... 1933 Frank C. Walker ... 1940	H. S. Cummings ... 1933 Frank Murphy..... 1939 Robert H. Jackson . 1940 Francis Biddle 1941	Elliot Lee Richardson... 1970 **SECRETARY OF HOUSING AND URBAN DEVELOPMENT**
James V. Forrestal. 1945*	Harold L. Ickes .... 1945 Julius C. Krug ..... 1946 Oscar L. Chapman . 1949	Frank C. Walker ... 1945 Robt. E. Hannegan . 1945 J. M. Donaldson ... 1947	Tom C. Clark...... 1945 J. H. McGrath..... 1949 J. P. McGranery ... 1952	Established September 9, 1965 Robert C. Weaver 1966
	Douglas McKay ... 1953 Fred A. Seaton 1956	A. E. Summerfield . 1953	H. Brownell, Jr. ... 1953 William P. Rogers.. 1957	Robert C. Wood .... 1969 George W. Romney 1969
	Stewart L. Udall ... 1961	J. Edward Day .... 1961 John A. Gronouski. 1963	Robert F. Kennedy . 1961	**SECRETARY OF TRANSPORTATION**
	Stewart L. Udall ... 1963 Walter J. Hickel.... 1969 Rogers C. B. Morton 1970	John A. Gronouski . 1963 Lawrence O'Brien .. 1965 W. Marvin Watson.. 1968 Winton M. Blount .. 1969	Robert F. Kennedy . 1963 Nicholas Katzen- back .... 1964 W. Ramsey Clark .. 1967 John N. Mitchell.... 1969	Established October 15, 1966 Alan S. Boyd ....1967 John A. Volpe 1969

*On March 4, 1913, the Department of Commerce and Labor was divided into the Department of Commerce and the Department of Labor.

INDEX

FOR ALL 16 VOLUMES

PAGE NUMBERS FOR EACH VOLUME

VOL. 1:	1–89 **E1–E37**	VOL. 5:	360–449 **E149–E185**	VOL. 9:	720–809 **E297–E333**	VOL. 13:	1080–1169 **E445–E481**
VOL. 2:	90–179 **E38–E74**	VOL. 6:	450–539 **E186–E222**	VOL. 10:	810–899 **E334–E370**	VOL. 14:	1170–1259 **E482–E518**
VOL. 3:	180–269 **E75–E111**	VOL. 7:	540–629 **E223–E259**	VOL. 11:	900–989 **E371–E407**	VOL. 15:	1260–1349 **E519–E555**
VOL. 4:	270–359 **E112–E148**	VOL. 8:	630–719 **E260–E296**	VOL. 12:	990–1079 **E408–E444**	VOL. 16:	1350–1416 **E556–E604**

Bold-face numerals indicate Encyclopedic Section pages